THEY'LL NEVER DO IT!

But volunteers did restore Stotfold
Watermill and created a Nature Reserve

by
Pamela Manfield and Trevor Radford

First published by Stotfold Mill Preservation Trust 2014

Copyright: Stotfold Mill Preservation Trust

ISBN 978-0-9928899-0-6

Design, layout and photo-enhancing: Barrie Dack and Associates
01462 834640
Print production by Managed Services, Once Upon a Time,
30 Gt Pulteney Street, London W1F 9NN
020 7534 8809

All rights reserved. Without limiting the rights under copyright reserved above, no part of this publication may be reproduced, stored or introduced into a retrieval system, or transmitted in any form or by any means (electronic, mechanical, photocopying, recording or otherwise), without the prior written permission of both the copyright owners and publisher of this book.

Pamela Manfield and Trevor Radford have asserted their rights to be identified as the authors of this work.

Front cover: The skeletal remains and the restored Stotfold Watermill from the Nature Reserve (Robert Smith)

Back cover: The Mill and Nature Reserve in winter

DEDICATION

'Keeping the wheels of history turning through the power of volunteers' is the official motto of Stotfold Watermill and Nature Reserve.

Without thousands of hours of volunteer time the Mill would not have been saved or restored, the Nature Reserve would not have been created – and neither would be sustainable. This book is, therefore, dedicated to all the volunteers, past, present and future, those who started, and those who keep, the wheels of history turning.

We hope it is both a faithful record of what took place and a fitting tribute.

Stotfold Watermill in the 1880s

The restored Mill proudly flying the flag of the Society for the Protection of Ancient Buildings (Mills Section)

CONTENTS

Part I	Starting the wheels of history turning	vii
Chapter One	Only a charred wreck remained	1
Chapter Two	One hundred eels and a worrying letter	7
Chapter Three	Four generations of Randalls	14
Chapter Four	First hopes of restoration	25
Chapter Five	Black as hell we were	37
Chapter Six	Rebuilding tested all my skills	46
Chapter Seven	Machinery magic	52
Chapter Eight	Stotfold Mill Preservation Trust and grant applications	79
Chapter Nine	Stotfold Watermill Local Nature Reserve and Teasel	86
Part II	Keeping the wheels of history turning	97
Chapter Ten	The Archive Team	99
Chapter Eleven	The Education Programme and the Guides Team	107
Chapter Twelve	Friends of the Mill and Millers Wheel	115
Chapter Thirteen	Information Technology and the website	122
Chapter Fourteen	The Kingfisher Gift Shop and flour sales	125
Chapter Fifteen	Local fundraising and major events	129
Chapter Sixteen	Marketing and the Small Events Team	142
Chapter Seventeen	The Milling and Maintenance Team	147
Chapter Eighteen	Randalls Tea Room	153
Chapter Nineteen	Stotfold Art Group	159
Chapter Twenty	Awards and recognition	162

John Hyde putting final touches to the running red fox weathervane

The new skeleton of the building starts to take shape

ACKNOWLEDGEMENTS

The authors would like to thank all those who gave their time to be interviewed, who sourced documents or photographs, and who read and checked facts.

We are particularly grateful to the following:

- ✧ Scilla Douglas and Pauline Humphries of Hitchin Historical Society for editing and advice.
- ✧ Stotfold Mill Archive Group: Keith Reynolds, Roger Watson and Richard Whitelock for sourcing and scanning documents and photographs and especially Carolyn Monaghan for her researches, which added so much detail to the chapters relating to the Mill's history and the Randall family.
- ✧ Lynn Roper for giving us access to her work log of the restoration and Jan Radford for allowing us to use items from her collection of Mill memorabilia.
- ✧ Geoff Hoile for allowing us to use his diagrams of the machinery.
- ✧ Bert Hyde and his family for permission to quote from his books on the history of Stotfold
- ✧ Jan Radford and Larry Stoter for proof reading.
- ✧ Many of the photographs have been donated to the Mill Archive over the years and it has been extremely difficult to attribute specific images to particular photographers. We are very grateful to the many people who have contributed wonderful images, especially Valerie Balderstone, Lucy Clarke, Frances and Gordon Huckle, Jean Kersey, Pam Manfield, Sarah Martin, Louden Masterton, Jan, Phil and Trevor Radford, Keith Reynolds, Lynn and Ron Roper, Robert Smith, Larry Stoter, Lorelie and Robin Tasker, Mike Thomas.

We are also grateful to the following for permission to use material:

Biggleswade Chronicle

English Heritage

Hertfordshire Archives and Local Studies

Society for the Protection of Ancient Buildings (SPAB) Mills Section

Stotfold Town Council

Streets Publishers for permission to quote from *'Stotfold Reflections'*

DISCLAIMER

We have tried to acknowledge all photographers, but in some cases this has not been possible. If anyone feels their photograph has been used without acknowledgement, please contact the Mill, so this information can be added to the Mill Archive and we will endeavour to add their name to reprinted versions of the book. Where the copyright owner is unknown, or if we have inadvertently overlooked any individual's copyright, we apologise.

We have done our utmost to ensure that all those who have been involved in helping restore or sustain the Mill and Nature Reserve are included. If anyone feels they have been omitted, please contact the Mill and we will endeavour to remedy this in future editions.

Whilst every effort has been made to ensure the accuracy of this work, it is a collection of people's memories. It is inevitable, therefore, with the passage of time, that there may be some variances in these. All recollections, views and opinions are those of the individuals indicated and not necessarily those of the authors.

Part I: STARTING THE WHEELS OF HISTORY TURNING

Today, Stotfold Watermill stands majestically astride the sleepy River Ivel as it has done for centuries. It seems impossible as one walks around this fascinating working watermill that, as late as 1997, the Mill was a gutted, soot-blackened, seemingly-doomed ruin and could so easily have remained like that.

We wrote this book to pay tribute to, and record in detail, the huge amount of work and vast optimism of the people who have saved the Mill - from those who shifted the very first barrow of ash, to those who continue to ensure the building's financial future is assured. It also records the work of those who have lovingly created the award-winning Nature Reserve that sits beside the Mill complex.

Throughout we have used, wherever possible, the words and recollections of those who were there. Sometimes, through the mists of time memories of details and events vary, so the reader may find the need to forgive the occasional inconsistency.

We set out to record how - starting with a handful of people and the desolate remains of a once-thriving business and historic machinery - Stotfold Mill rose like a phoenix from the ashes, reaching a point where hundreds of volunteers are the life blood of a building that has, since opening to the public, attracted tens of thousands of visitors, including The Duke of Edinburgh and The Duke of Kent. It has been the subject of television documentaries and won prestigious awards including the Queen's Award for Voluntary Service. The Mill and Nature Reserve have become well-known and highly-regarded examples of heritage preservation, provide a much-valued and much-used educational resource and are above all a source of great civic pride in the quiet little town of Stotfold, which they have done so much to put on the map. It is our hope that this book will ensure this important chapter in the Mill's story is preserved forever.

The Mill has been at the centre of life in Stotfold for a millennium or more. We didn't want to lose it and we are very, very proud of it. As the Duke of Edinburgh remarked on his visit, "Well, it's your town!" And that's the point. We could have let the Mill go, it could have been one more fading photograph on a pub wall, but instead, against seemingly-impossible odds, this wonderful building and machinery were saved, and a beautiful Nature Reserve created. Perhaps someday, someone will read this book and be encouraged to feel that they too can take on a seemingly lost cause in their town or village - and succeed.

This is the story of how Stotfold Watermill was saved and the Nature Reserve created...

The end wall was all that was left standing

A view of the ruins from the neighbouring garden, with wildlife visitors

CHAPTER ONE

ONLY A CHARRED WRECK REMAINED

The night of Tuesday, 14th December 1992 was cold and windy, but the residents of the small Bedfordshire town of Stotfold were sleeping peacefully, presumably dreaming – according to age – of Christmas presents or Christmas preparations. In the early hours of the 15th, Julian Tasker, whose bedroom was at the back of Mill House, two doors along from Stotfold Mill, was awoken by the frantic honking of the family geese, Dan and Doris. He heard a great gushing noise, saw flames flickering past the window and dashed to wake his brother and sister and then his parents.

Lorelie Tasker remembered, *"Julian woke me by pulling me out of bed, shouting, 'Get out! The Mill's on fire.' We went to stand on the other side of the road, in our night clothes and wellington boots – in December. The fire was very dramatic and affected us all very badly. I had nightmares about it for years and our daughter, Roxane, who was eleven at the time, became very concerned about the safety of open fires. I hope never to have to cope with something like that ever again."*

For some time before the blaze, the family had been very concerned about the dangers posed by the derelict Mill and Robin Tasker had kept an eye on the building, regularly clearing out intruders as he was worried that they might be hurt or would set fires.

Before she left the house, Lorelie dialled 999 and a fire engine arrived in less than ten minutes, *"though it felt like hours. The entire Mill was on fire, grass and riverbank, the big yews in the garden and the flames were licking at the building beside the house. It was heart-breaking as we knew the Mill so well, and loved the fact it was in absolutely original condition."*

When the first fire engine arrived, the crew quickly decided that one tender could not cope with the blaze, so an additional four engines were eventually called to deal with the inferno. These included one from Kempston, with a large hydraulic platform, since it was clear the only way to deal with the fire was from above. There was no chance

Chapter One

of saving Stotfold Watermill, which was alight from end to end, but it was hoped at least the hoses could play water on the nearby dwellings and prevent them from being destroyed. This became the priority, as the guttering on Mill Cottage was starting to singe and there was already slight damage to the roof of Mill House. Luckily for the fire crews and the residents of the adjoining dwellings, the wind was coming from downstream and this limited the spread of the flames towards the buildings.

Paul Mackin, who was officer in charge at Shefford Fire Station at the time of the fire, took control of the operation till approximately 4.00 am when a more senior officer arrived. His log recalls the details of call number 7044, timed at 03.23 hours. Nine firemen were sent from Shefford. Besides Paul Mackin, these included John Brown; Peter Cooper; Damien Standring; Colin Meredith; Nick Teer; Nigel Keeping; Keven (sic) Meeks and Martin Steele. These men fought the fire until 7.45 am, when they *'left the scene under the control of the Duty Supervisory Officer'.*

In total, 27 firemen helped fight the fire and Paul recalled, "*Whenever local fire fighters get together to swing the lamp and talk of major fires, Stotfold Watermill is one of those iconic fires that figures most often. We could see the flames lighting up the night sky as we were coming up Hitchin Hill into Stotfold. The 65 foot high chimney, which had a distinct lean, became our main concern, so one fireman was detailed just to keep an eye on it until daylight. It was possible that the fire might have been started by an intruder who could still be in the building, so I went along the alleyway between the buildings, to take a recce to check if anyone was inside. It was very dark and there was lots of smoke and it was obvious it was much too dangerous to go further inside. The upper floors were well alight and I could get no further than the ground floor.*"

As the Tasker family stood outside, in the cold December night, in disbelief and shock, Lorelie Tasker kept thinking, "*If Julian had not woken up, the top of the house would have fallen in on us.*" She recalled, "The geese, which had probably saved our lives, had to be shut in the greenhouse to prevent them attacking the firemen. Roxane's pet hamster was rescued by a fireman, but the cats – sensibly – disappeared."

Flames were roaring twenty to thirty feet high, across both adjoining properties. The family watched in horror as the overhanging luccam fell into the road and the wooden seat across the road spontaneously burst into flame. There were loud splashes as several of the heavy, cast-iron hursting columns fell into the river. It was later discovered the heat had been so intense that a mirror on the wall in Mill Cottage had melted.

Lorelie said, *"The houses were saved by the river. The fire engines only had limited water, so they got into the grounds of Stotfoldbury and one fire engine filled up at the front and then put pumps into the river. Without this water they could not have coped".* Paul Mackin agreed, *"It was lucky we could use the river for water as we only had 400 gallons and this was used quickly as the fire was going so well."*

Lorelie continued, *"We later heard that they could see the flames as far away as Biggleswade; all we could do was watch this inferno so close to our home."* They were not allowed back in to their house until early morning, by which time they were *"pretty chilly and hungry."*

Freda Stevenson, who lived opposite the Mill, was woken by the unusual noises outside and looked out to see the road covered with fire engines and police cars. However, despite the number of appliances called to the scene, most other local residents were totally unaware of the drama taking place in Mill Lane.

The cold, grey light of morning revealed that the four-storey, weatherboarded building which had dominated Stotfold for so many years had been reduced to a heap of smouldering ash and rubble, with only the jagged remnants of the end walls still standing. Even these did not remain for long, as the Fire Chief insisted that they had to be taken down for safety reasons, especially the wall between the Mill and Mill Cottage. The adjoining cottage wall was only lath and plaster, which had been played with water continuously to stop it burning

Firemen spraying water over the smouldering remains

Chapter One

Charred timbers littered the road outside while (below) can be seen the damaged parts of the sack hoist mechanism and iron columns, much of which would eventually be salvaged and reinstated

and the brick wall could have fallen through, or onto passing vehicles or people. So, scaffolding turned up on Monday and the walls were demolished. Lorelie Tasker said, "*It was so sad the end wall had to come down, as that was the only bit left of the whole building and it had helped protect our houses.*"

She recalled, "*Robin spent the whole of the morning after the fire on the phone, attempting to save the Mill for future generations by contacting any organisations he hoped might be able to help or give advice.*" Despite the concerns of the fire brigade that the ruined Mill was not safe, he also went into the building "*with dustpan, brush and bucket*" to see what he could do to clear the area. Debris and ash were shoulder-height and still smouldering. "*That's how determined he was,*" Lorelie said.

Gordon Huckle, who like many of the local lads had worked in the Mill on summer holidays and weekends, was stunned by the sight of the ruined building. "*It had been part of our lives and now it was in a hell of a state. I had heard about attempts to revive the Mill, but I thought, 'It's had it now'. The fire engine was still there damping things down and it looked a real charred mess.*"

Sam Randall, whose family had owned the Mill for nearly a century and who had finally been forced to sell as the business became uneconomic, was very upset. Even after he had sold the business, he used to cycle past the Mill every day and Lorelie Tasker remembered thinking, "*What on earth will Sam think? The whole history of his family was gone.*" Gordon Huckle recalled, "*Sam was in a terrible way after the fire. He couldn't speak to anyone. The Mill had been his life.*" Sam later admitted that it was a long time before he could bear to go past the ruined building.

Local farmer Frank Hyde said, "*After the fire, even the tar on the road in front of the Mill had melted. Everything was smoking and smouldering. The central shaft was standing there scorched and reminded me of the poem of the Ancient Mariner.*" His wife, Jane, remembered looking out from her bedroom window first thing that morning and thinking that something about the Mill chimney looked wrong. She said, "*We had been worried about the Mill burning down for a while as there had been a number of minor arson incidents and we knew intruders were getting in.*" When she took the dogs out across the field later, she saw the full extent of the damage. "*A group of us stood outside the ruin saying, 'We can't just let the building go'.*" She also remembered, "*The hand-made nails had flown out all over the road; we picked them up for days afterwards.*"

Sheila Archer was then the local postwoman. She recalled, "*I went down Mill Lane on the morning after the fire, doing my postal deliveries.*

Chapter One

The skeletal remains

The police were stopping people from going further, but I explained I had to deliver letters to Stotfoldbury, opposite the Mill and they let me through. I was so angry; the Mill was a real mess and the fire engines were still there. I still feel really strongly about it twenty years later."

Alan Stoyel of the Mills Section of the Society for the Protection of Ancient Buildings visited the Mill after the fire, in order to make a report. *"It was a freezing cold day and I spent this recording the damage and taking photos, some of which have snow and ice in them. It was a filthy, black, dreadful job."*

David Baker, then Conservation Officer for Bedfordshire County Council, with responsibility for listed buildings was quoted as saying, *"The whole wooden structure of the mill was damaged beyond repair. It is still a listed building, however, because there is a lot of 19th century machinery in there. It is sad to see this once superb building looking so bad."*

The report in the local newspaper – *The Biggleswade Chronicle* – underlined the tragic events that had taken place: '*A two-hundred year old mill was razed to the ground after fire swept through its 18th century timber frame. Now all that remains of the once proud landmark situated on the River Ivel in Stotfold is a charred wreck.*'

CHAPTER TWO

ONE HUNDRED EELS AND A WORRYING LETTER

Grinding seeds, grains or nuts to make them edible is an ancient activity, going back to prehistoric hunter-gatherers. Two pieces of stone were used; the bottom one was stationary and could be quite large, while the upper stone in the form of a pestle was used to smash and grind the items down. Often stones found in ancient settlements and along the tracks of migrations would be used over many generations and in some places, like North America, some large flat stones can still be seen, pock-marked with many smaller grinding pockets.

As societies became more settled, farming of grain developed and the first querns appeared. They still used a stationary bottom stone, but had a hole drilled in the top (handstone) to take the grain and this upper stone, as can be inferred from the name, was rotated by hand. This technique made grinding much more efficient and stones like this can still be found in use in places in the developing world today.

The Greeks invented the two main components of watermills – the waterwheel and toothed gearing – and, with the Romans, were the first to operate undershot, overshot and breastshot water wheels by about the third century BC. The first technical description of a watermill is sometime between 40-10 BC by Vitruvius, a Roman engineer. This mill was fitted with an undershot wheel and power transferred by a linked gearing mechanism. Between 20 BC -10 AD, Antipater of Thessalonica described an advanced overshot wheel, which he praised for its efficiency in grinding corn and the reduction of human labour. The Romans are believed to have introduced the concept of modern water mills into Britain.

Bedstone mortar, Indian Grinding Rock State Historic Park, Sierra Nevada, California

Chapter Two

Nobody is certain of the exact date, but it is likely that a watermill has stood on the site of the current Stotfold Mill beside the River Ivel for over a thousand years and it is certainly one of the oldest recorded buildings in the town. The first written evidence is the mention of four mills in Stotfold in the Domesday Book of 1086, commissioned by William the Conqueror to ensure taxes were levied on his newly-conquered land. One of those four was the currently-named Stotfold Mill. The combined rents, payable to Hugh de Beauchamp, Baron of Bedford, was £4 and four hundred eels. (Eels were a valuable food item at the time.) 103 mills were listed in Bedfordshire and milling was a manorial monopoly; peasants were forced to take their grain to the lord's mills to be ground into flour.

The name of the Mill varied over the years; it was called Randall's Mill at various times, after the family who ran it from 1873. In a map of 1765 it is referred to as the Upper Mill. It was also known as the Old Mill, but the Post Office Directory of 1869 and delivery notes issued by the Randalls themselves refer to Stotfold Mill, which name has been retained to the present day.

The Mill changed hands many times over the centuries, with each change of ownership or tenancy being ratified by the court of the Lord of Brayes Manor. Details were entered onto a court roll, hence the term 'tenancy by copyhold'. The earliest record is in 1406, when John and Alice Wedewessen granted the Mill to John's brother, Simon and on 5th April 1516 we know that Richard Lorymer took over ownership from Peter Thorp. The next important date is 1694 when John Guilbert (or Gilbird) rented the Mill from James Saunders (or Sanders), paying 25 shillings rent and a heriot of the same amount. A heriot was a fine due to the lord of the manor on the death of a tenant. The historical record then becomes less clear, but in 1707, included in the list of lands and tithes belonging to Stotfold Vicarage, were the *'two watermills in the parish, each of which pays the Vicar ten shillings per annum'*.

When John Guilbert died on 13th June 1715, his wife Anne and son John inherited the mill. On 2nd October 1734, Anne's grandson, William Guilbert of Lemsford Mill inherited three quarters of the property, only getting the final quarter share on 3rd May, 1740 when he became 21, from his Aunt Isabella Templeman – Anne's daughter – and her husband. Since the Guilbert family already were millers, it is believed they employed a tenant miller at Stotfold, probably James Woodward.

Henry Dawson then bought the Mill on 22nd July 1757, though he only owned it for a short time, moving to London to become a *'gentleman's servant'* on 23rd March 1767. Francis Smith then owned the property, though he apparently came very close to losing it. The Hertfordshire Archives and Local Studies section holds a letter of 25th December 1770 from William Bennett in London explaining the precarious position:

> *This is to inform you that though a stranger to me you may expect to be involved in trouble by law in a very little time except you can find the means to avoid the suit you will certainly have young Woodward lay claim to your mill by virtue of a deed and surrender dated 22nd March 1739. In the deed Wm. Gilbird of Lemsford who owned your mill bound himself to a bond of £250 to pay to Jane Gilbird for 30 years the sum of £10 per annum and on her death to pay to her administrators £120.*
>
> *She has since died and the deed is now in the hands of her grandson, Mr Woodward. You will find him troublesome as he wants your mill to live in. You bought the mill from Mr Dawson but Mr Woodward's surrender is prior to that which Mr Dawson bought the mill from Thorp you will find his title in law will stand good before yours unless you pay him £120. He has the advice of a number of first class lawyers and they give it as their opinion to be his right. Now he has sent to the steward of the court to know when there will be a court day that he may come and deal with the matter.*
>
> *Should you require it you may depend on my assistance at any time. You can get in touch with me by leaving a letter at the General Post Office in Lombard Street.*
>
> *I am Sir your very humble servant to command*
>
> William Bennett

As Bert Hyde notes in his book, *The Mills of Stotfold*, 'a rather strange letter to write on Christmas Day. Obviously Mr Bennett was a hard working solicitor touting for business.' The Woodwards and Gilbirds or Guilberts were closely related and had owned the mill for a long time. In fact young Woodward's father, James, had been miller there, so it had been the family home at one time.

Francis Smith somehow managed to hold on to the Mill until his death in 1781, when he left it to his wife, Alice, and his son and daughter, John and Mary, who ran the business jointly for the next seven years. Mary married Thomas Gurney and by September 1793 the Mill was being run by the two Gurneys and Mary's brother, John. Following John's death and then Mary's, Thomas managed the Mill until his nephew (also named John) came of age. On 25th February 1800, John became 21 and promptly sold his share of the Mill to Thomas who ran it for the next 24 years.

Chapter Two

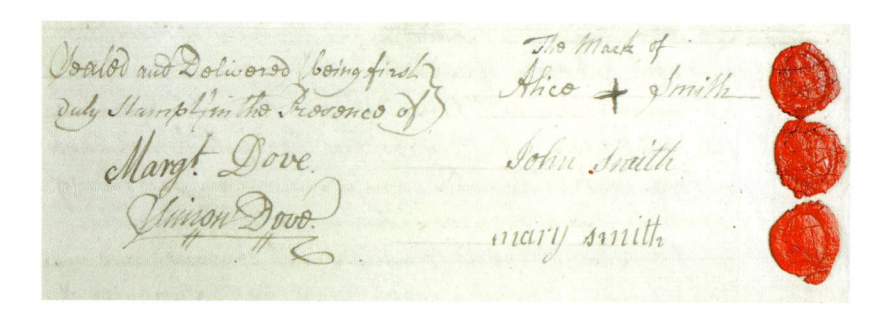

A legal document showing the Smith family signatures. Note that Alice Smith cannot write her name, so puts a cross

On 11th October 1824, the Mill was sold to James Pestell, formerly a miller in Radwell, for £1,700. James borrowed the money from his former employer at Radwell Mill, aptly named Samuel Mills, though Mills was not a working man, but a *'gentleman'*, living in Russell Square in London.

A great fire destroyed the Mill in 1825 and Pestell was forced to rebuild. The new building had four storeys, the lower one in yellow gault bricks – Stotfold Stocks – from the nearby Wrayfields brick kiln and the top floors covered in weather boarding. From 1828 onwards mortgages and loans were taken out to cover costs and from February

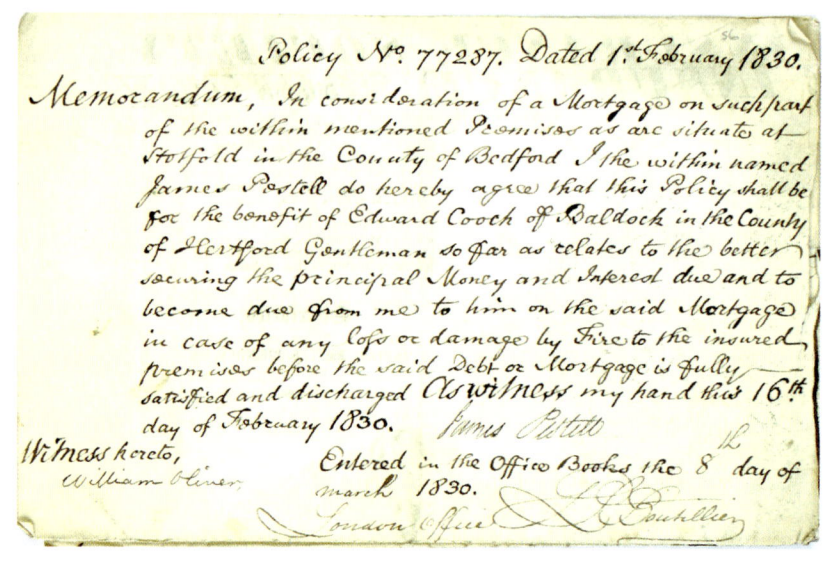

A document from 1830, bearing James Pestell's signature

1830 the Mill was covered by newly-introduced fire insurance for the very first time. The Norwich Union Fire Insurance Company insured the new Mill for £5,200 at an annual premium of £29.16s. £1,800 represented the Mill itself, with £500 for contents, including *'a waterwheel, standing and going gear, a dressing machine, five pairs of stones, but seldom working more than four pair at one time.'* The remainder of the insurance valuation represented the adjoining house and contents, offices and stables, barns, pigsties, plus various implements, animals and stock in trade.

However, the rebuilding proved too great a strain on Pestell's finances, so on the 10th of January 1831, the Mill and contents were sold to pay his debtors. Around April 1831, he was evicted and William Hogg and Robert Lindsell (local solicitors) were made interim administrators, with William Cane and John Taylor working as millers. Pestell was finally declared bankrupt on 3rd February 1832 and the business was later sold to George Waldock. Like other millers who got into financial problems, living a life of luxury may have been much to blame. The inventory of his possessions listed two large mahogany tables with 16 chairs; Brussels carpets; Venetian blinds; ornate fireplaces and furnishings, including household linens, silks, silver cutlery and cut glass items. On the ground floor he had a large, well-equipped kitchen; a brew house with coppers and mash tubs; a cellar with barrels of beer and a wine store. The six bedrooms boasted feather beds, brass bedsteads and mahogany furniture, while even the garret bedrooms for the servants were luxuriously furnished. In the stables were five horses, a wagon, three carts and a gig – an impressive list for a country miller in a small town.

George Waldock, born in Stotfold, but then living at Astwick Mill, bought Stotfold Mill for £3,400 on 6th November 1841. He was already engaged in farming, brickmaking and running two other mills, so he employed a journeyman miller – Joseph Cole – to oversee the business in Stotfold, with Thomas

Joseph Cole, miller at Stotfold Mill in 1841

Chapter Two

Gurney as an apprentice. (Cole, who lived next door in Mill House with his wife and five daughters, later moved to become miller at Tempsford Mill, also on the River Ivel.)

George Waldock died in 1854, leaving half shares in both Astwick and Stotfold Mills to his youngest sons David and Henry, though the latter then sold his half of Stotfold Mill to David for *'a consideration'*

The Mill in the 1880s

of £25. David Waldock paid off his father's debts of £3,000 and, once the Manor Court had ratified all the deals in 1859, embarked on a series of improvements to Stotfold Mill.

On 10th June 1861, he bought some land behind the Mill alongside the river from a London silversmith, John Jones Vaughan for £100. Crucially, this was freehold property and so out of the control of the Manor Court. On this land, directly behind the Mill, where the Tea Room now stands, Waldock installed a steam engine made by Varty and Company of Royston and a Lancashire boiler. He also undertook the erection of the 65 foot high chimney, which served the boiler, at the back of the Mill. The signature of H Waldock, at the base of the chimney is probably David's brother Henry. Two millers lived at the Mill and worked for Waldock: John Taylor and his nephew Charles Gayler. However, despite his improvements, the business obviously did not pay, as David Waldock was declared bankrupt on 18th March,1863, when the land, Mill House, the Mill and all its contents were sold to pay his 35 creditors. One of these was a young John Randall, who was later to take over the Mill and run it successfully.

David received £25 by way of support for his family. The custom of the Manor Court was to hand over a token piece of furniture to represent the forfeited goods: David chose a whip. Sadly, his fortunes declined further. By 1871 he was living with his children and new wife, Sarah Ann, in a tenement in East London on the East India Dock Road and working as a dock labourer. He finally returned to Stotfold and died in 1877, aged only 46.

William Vaughan, a member of a prominent local family who owned Manor and Grange Farms, bought the Mill for £4,150 on 30th January 1863, though the tenancy passed to his son William Thomas on 15th November, 1869. The Vaughans also did not run the business themselves, but leased it out to a tenant – Samuel Garret – who lived at the Mill and employed two men. His foreman, William Sarl, who also lived at the Mill was *"a stonemason as well as a miller and as such was very useful in a mill that had grinding stones,"* as Bert Hyde comments.

In 1873 John Randall became the tenant miller. After William Thomas Vaughan's death on 10th August, 1886, his children inherited as 'tenants in common'. They obviously did not wish to run the business as on 31st May 1887, it was put up for sale as *'a very valuable estate on the river Rhee'* (an old name for the River Ivel). John Randall bought it for £2,000, on 24th March 1888, though it took until 14th November 1896 for the sale to be finally ratified by the Manor Court. The Randall family ran the Mill until 1966 when it ceased business, though they retained ownership until 1984.

CHAPTER THREE

FOUR GENERATIONS OF RANDALLS

The Randalls were an old Stotfold family, appearing in parish records from the early seventeenth century. The first member for whom there are detailed records was John, born in 1784 to William and Mary Randall and brought up as a general Baptist, though he later became a Strict Baptist. At first he was a farm labourer, earning ten shillings a week, but his standing in the local community is shown by the fact that he was one of the local militia called out to control the rioters during the notorious Stotfold Riots of 1830. (The 'rioters' were in fact mainly agricultural labourers merely asking for better conditions of work.)

By 1834 John was successful enough to be able to buy his own cottage and an adjoining one in Queen Street. The family were obviously well-known for being hard working, thrifty and independent, as in 1835, Randall was awarded a two pounds and ten shillings prize by the Bedfordshire Agricultural Society. The award recognised that despite being only a labourer, he had managed to bring up ten children without having recourse to parish relief.

John Randall later became a postmaster and finally a straw product manufacturer. By 1851 he employed five women and a boy in the local straw plait industry. The plaiting of straw and making these plaits into hats was a prominent rural occupation in Bedfordshire in the 18th and 19th centuries, reaching its peak in the 1870s, after which cheaper imports from China, and later Japan, forced the industry into decline. Bedfordshire corn straw had the right consistency to enable it to be worked easily without splitting and the finished straw plaits were sold on to the markets in Hitchin or Luton. Christine Smith's book '*Stotfold Reflections*' details the activity involved:

> *The men were mostly responsible for growing and cutting the straw and would sell it on to dealers who purchased the unthrashed stacks of wheat. The best and largest stems were selected and stripped to remove the knots and leaf, sorted and tied into bundles. After cutting, the straw went through a bleaching process.*

Plaiting was an ideal occupation for women and young children because it could be done at home. The children were sent to plait school almost as soon as they could walk generally working in very poor conditions. In the 1851 Census for Stotfold, Jane Gentle, Mary Gentle and Elizabeth Cooper were all listed as 'mistress of a school for straw plait only'. In the mid 1800s, a wife and two children could supplement the husband's agricultural wage of 10 shillings a week by an additional 12 shillings or more.

John died in 1862 and his wife, Sarah (née Bygrave) followed a year later.

The fourth of their ten children, named John after his father, was born on 20th June, 1828 into difficult times, but followed the family tradition of hard work. At the age of twelve, he was apprenticed to Jordan's Mill, near Biggleswade, then run by the Powers family, to be trained as a miller, at a wage of 8 shillings (40 pence) a week.

By the 1850s he had become a journeyman miller at nearby Stanford Mill and while living in Stanford met and married Elizabeth Lockey, who bore him seven children. Sadly, three of these died in infancy and Elizabeth herself passed away shortly after the last birth. A few years later John married her sister Hannah and a further six children were produced.

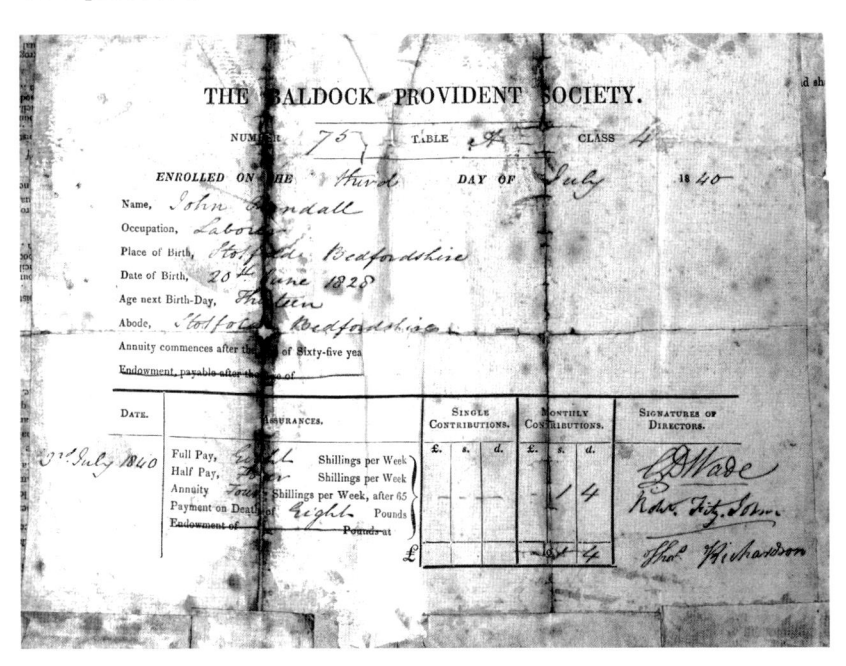

John Randall, aged 12 and a labourer, invests in his pension fund

Chapter Three

In the 1860s John started to buy farm land in and around Stotfold, especially at Radwell Grange. He took out several private mortgages for this and repaying them took many years. He also bought cottages in Arlesey Road and Brook Street and had inherited two cottages in Queen Street from his father, where he and the family were living in 1871. For many years he worked both as a baker (running a bakery in Brook Street), as well as being a farmer. By 1881 he owned seventeen cottages, farmed fifty acres of land and employed several men and boys. His son, also named John and a master baker later inherited the bakery, which he ran with his wife Elizabeth. As a prominent citizen of the town, he became a member of the first Stotfold Town Council formed in 1894.

The opportunity to rent Stotfold Mill from the Vaughan family arose in 1873 and John jumped at the chance, since the mill fitted in well with his other occupations, his two eldest sons were old enough to work as millers and Mill House was large enough for all the family. Two years after William Vaughan died in 1886, John bought the Mill, Mill House and some land for £2,000. This was under the manorial copyhold system (a type of leasehold) and he took out yet another

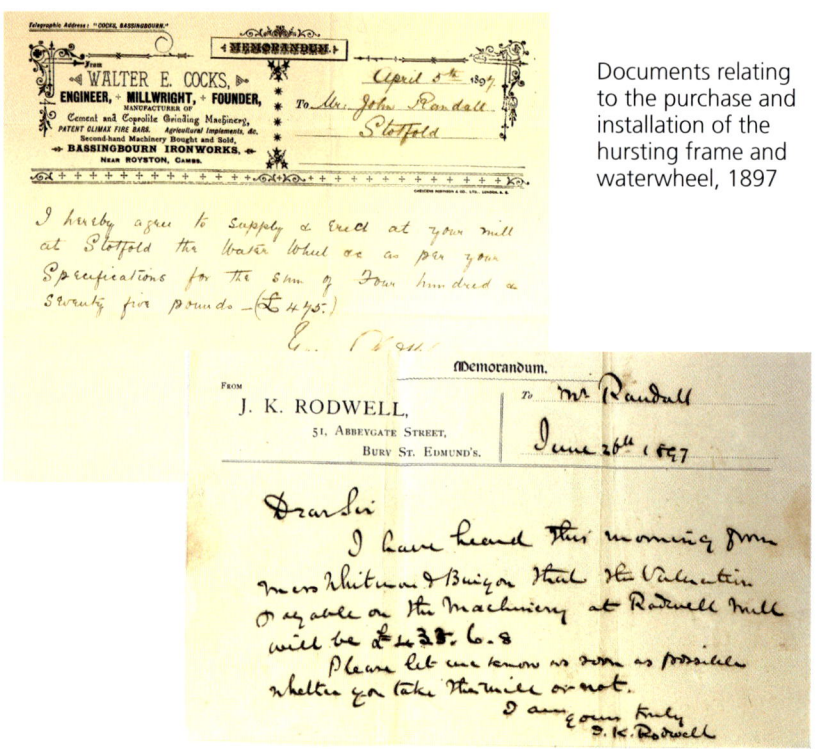

Documents relating to the purchase and installation of the hursting frame and waterwheel, 1897

mortgage for this purchase. He also started an ambitious programme of improvements including the addition of three pairs of engine stones, which were under-driven from a shaft that ran along the back wall. He also extended the mill building to cover this and installed a new Robinson's separator – used to clean grain before milling – on the first floor.

In 1897, a new waterwheel, designed by John Lampit of Hemel Hempstead, was built and probably installed by Walter E Cocks of Bassingbourn. This wheel was the maximum width possible in the space available – over fourteen feet wide – and is the widest in a corn mill in the United Kingdom. There was also a new pit wheel made by J Burroughs of Clophill. Most importantly for the future of the Mill restoration, a cast-iron hursting frame by Whitmore and Binyon was installed in 1898. Whitmore and Binyon, of Wickham Market in Suffolk, who were in business from 1780 until 1901 had built a reputation for making extremely high quality mill equipment. It is believed this hursting was originally installed in Radwell Mill and moved to Stotfold. There is an estimate in the Mill Archive for this work, but no furtherdocumentary evidence in support.

All these improvements were expensive and John constantly re-mortgaged properties and

Ebenezer Randall as a young man and (below) the Randall family at leisure in the 1890s

Chapter Three

land to pay for them. Competition from roller mills, including the six small roller mills established at Bowman's in Astwick, was increasing, so he also drew up plans to convert some buildings on his land, then being used as a granary, to a large, modern roller mill.

Unfortunately, John Randall died in 1900 before his plans could be implemented. At probate, his personal estate was valued at £5,351 10s 6d and his business at £8,075 5s 9d – large sums of money for a country farmer and miller, particularly considering his modest beginnings. In the late 1800s a new cemetery had opened in Mill Lane, Stotfold and John had bought two of the first plots at the very top of a small hill. Hannah died only a year after her husband and the spot where they are buried overlooks Stotfold and the Mill where they spent most of their lives.

On John's death the Mill was left to his son, Ebenezer, who was born at Mill House in 1872 and inherited the property at the age of twenty-eight. John also left him all the outbuildings and land, the milling equipment, a wagon, carts, harnesses, dog carts, two horses and a nag. His mother left him the household effects and furniture when she died nine months later, so he was well set up to make his living as the next miller at the start of the 20th century.

In 1902 he carried out his father's ambitious plan to build a roller mill next door; local builders, Redhouse, were employed at a cost of £1,200. Unfortunately, Stotfold Mill and all the small local watermills were adversely affected by the new large roller mill built by Bowman's opposite Hitchin Station and completed in 1901. This new building housed six roller mills each producing three and a half sacks of flour an hour. The simpler system enabling huge quantities of grain to be milled quickly, plus the faster distribution, directly from the farms to the mill and then loading the flour onto trains, meant smaller mills were no longer economic.

In 1907 Ebenezer married Gertrude Myatt Johnson from Ulverston, Lancashire. Sadly, two days before Christmas, their first child Margaret died at only four days old, but three more children were born in Stotfold and lived at Mill House. Ebenezer was something of a country gentleman and enjoyed the sports of fishing and shooting, the latter accompanied by one of his dogs, a field spaniel called Stotfold Rex, which was famous locally as *'a real sportsman's dog'*.

Ebenezer still had the family farming interests and later bought up farm stock to work eleven acres of arable land and, as well as farming and carrying on the business of a mill, in the early 1920s he also bought Twelvetrees – a bankrupt bakery in Biggleswade. Perhaps this was a venture too far, as he was forced to file for bankruptcy in 1928. A depression in the milling trade was partly to blame, but more critical was the failure of the farming venture with nephew John Warren Randall, who had worked as a pigman and mealman but had run into debt. To try to help him, in 1918 his uncle Ebenezer set him up in a 320 acre arable farm in Arrington, Cambridgeshire and provided him with £2,000 to clear his debts. Though the farm was at first successful, it had to be sold in 1927. These failures, combined with the guaranteeing of his brother William's debts, the debts his father had left and the expenses for his wife's illness in the days before National Health Service treatment, left Ebenezer in a critical position, especially since he seemed unclear about his expenditure. The Official Receiver while trying to sort out his money problems, raised questions about his personal spending of £900 a year. *"Weren't you leading the life of a rich man?"* to which Ebenezer replied, *"No, I thought I was spending £4 per week."*

However with Trustees in charge of the estate, Ebenezer was able to carry on farming and milling. He continued to give special financial terms to his family, especially in the war years, as his ledger shows. He died at home in 1947 but Gertrude lived to the age of 87, ending her days in the Three Counties Asylum. They were both buried on the north side of Stotfold cemetery with the rest of the family, overlooking the family mill.

Frank Hyde, who used to work at the Mill in his school holidays, remembers Ebenezer (known as Eb) well. *"He was a real patriarch and came from a strict Baptist family – though he didn't go to chapel much. He was a sparely-built man, who could be very abrupt. He didn't believe in electricity as he thought this would burn them in their beds, so he used old storm lanterns filled with oil, one near the front door and one near the old coachhouse which he used as a garage."*

For most of his life Charles, John's third son, worked with his father at Randall's Mill, as it was then known. He married quite late in life at the age of forty-seven and had three children with Maud Lilla. By 1911 the census shows they were living in Rook Tree Lane and Charles stated he was '*of independent means*'. In his will, his father had left Charles a weekly amount of 12 shillings (60p) for life from the mill's profits. Maud ended her days in the Three Counties Asylum, aged 80, and both are buried in the old section of Stotfold Cemetery.

Not all of the Randalls were renowned for their hard work and business acumen. There was a William Randall in each generation from 1775 till the early 1900s, but Ebenezer's brother William was the black sheep of the family – in debt to his father at an early age. In 1882 John decided to take on the tenancy of Church Farm, Tadlow, Cambridgeshire. He encouraged William and his wife Eleanor to move

Chapter Three

there to work the land and try to repay the £3,658 they owed him. Sadly Eleanor died aged 31 after giving birth to her namesake. The two children were brought up by their grandmother, Hannah and the family at Randall's Mill, though they returned to their father in 1901 when Hannah died. William remarried after a few years, to Sara Jane from Ashwell. They had a further five boys and two girls and trying to support this large household only added to William's problems, though for a time he did seem to be succeeding.

He had been left ten acres of land in Stotfold (provided he cleared his debts) and he seemed to have redeemed himself enough so that his brother Ebenezer made him an executor to his will in 1922 and guaranteed his account with the bank in the same year. However, on William's death in 1928, the full extent of his debts became known; Ebenezer could not pay the bank and had to file for bankruptcy. Most of the Randall family, even those who moved away and their spouses, have been buried in prime positions in Stotfold Cemetery. William never returned and is buried in Tadlow.

A begging letter from William to his brother in 1922, asking him to provide security of £1,000 against his overdraft

Ebenezer had three children: Ruth Hilda, Frederick George and Samuel Leslie. George Shepherd, quoted in *"Stotfold Reflections"*, tells of his association with the family during Ebenezer's time: *"I left school, at 13 I think it was, and I went to work down Randall's Mill, 10 shillings a week. I had to clean the shoes for Ruth and George and I had to take them to school in a pony and cart. George went to school at Radwell, Reverend Waller was his schoolmaster, and Ruth went to Grove House School in Baldock. But I never fetched her home, her father had got an old T-Ford car and he used to bring her home.*

During the day I used to harness the donkey – they had a donkey as well – and go up and fetch a load of mangel-wurzels. They used to have a contraption that you put the

wurzels in one at a time, turn a handle and that ground them up and they mixed them up with the chaff, that was feed for the horses.

Another thing I used to do, they'd got a big machine in there and what he done was 'dress' corn. An old man named Freddy Gentle worked there. I used to have to turn the handle and he put the corn in. It used to blow all the dirt out of the corn. I had to collect the eggs up and Eb Randall, the miller, would come to me some mornings and say, 'Shepherd, there's a dozen duck eggs up the river, go and fetch them.' I used to have to wash these duck eggs ready for them to take to the Hitchin market and hens' eggs.

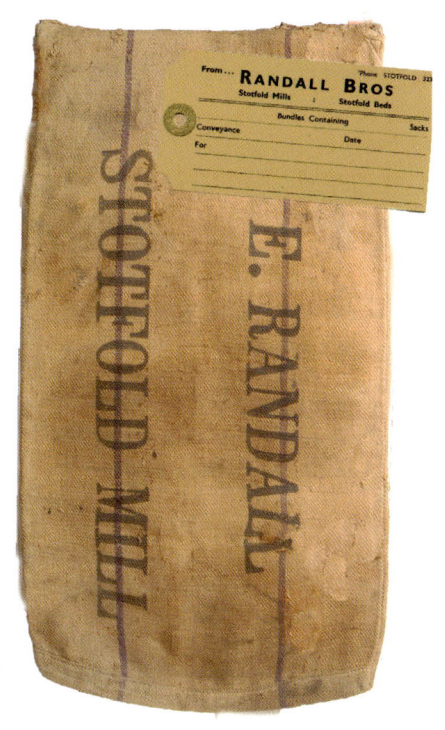

When I worked at the Mill there was Frank Bishop, he was the foreman and Frank Cooper was the labourer and there was two men in the Mill and two men on the horses and cart, Fred Gentle and me, that's all the men that worked there.

I used to like Eb Randall. I'd go shooting with him, doing the beating. We would go in his old Ford car.'

Items relating to the Randall's milling business

After Sam's birth when their mother became ill and was not around for most of their childhood, Ruth, who was the oldest, took over running the household, including the accounts, She had a fairly comfortable upbringing, was gifted as a pianist and in later life gave piano lessons. In recognition of her support, Ebenezer left her all his cars and the furniture for Mill House, which remained her home until it was sold in 1985. She died, aged 84, at 18 Queen Street in Stotfold.

George and Sam, were the last working millers at Randall's Mill. They had both joined the Home Guard in 1942, presumably exempt from military service as they were in a reserved occupation. After

Chapter Three

Ebenezer, Sam and George in August, 1927

their father's death, the three siblings inherited the Mill and ran it jointly from 1947. Chris Webster remembered as a girl in Arlesey how she had visited the Mill in the 1950s. Her father kept cows, pigs and horses and only liked to feed them with grain he had grown himself, so he always brought it to Stotfold Mill for grinding. Chris said, *"Sam was always so interested in the people who came to the Mill, not just about making money. Dad used to chat to him for ages. It was wonderful the Mill started working again while Sam was still alive."*

However, competition continued to increase from the faster and less expensive roller mills, especially the huge mills built near ports to grind the North American grain imported during and after World War II. In spite of installing a diesel engine in 1954 and switching to the production of animal foodstuffs, the Randalls were finally forced to cease milling in 1966. After that their main occupation and income was from farming. Sam had a lifelong love of cars and motorbikes and found work as a driver.

George became the only Randall of this generation to marry, at the advanced age of 47. Chris Webster recalled seeing the young George going off courting Malvene who lived at Poplar Farm. *"Every Sunday he used to bike down to the farm. You could set your clock by him"*. Despite his devoted attention Malvene married someone else, but

George Randall in front of the Roller Mill

after her first husband's death, she finally agreed to wed George. They were married in the lovely church of All Saints, Radwell and moved into Church Road, Stotfold. George Randall died aged 82, shortly before the Mill burned down in 1992. Malvene, who died in September 2004, obviously loved the Mill too, as she left a legacy of £27,000 for its support.

After the sale of the Mill, Sam Randall moved to a cottage at Wrayfields in1985. He lived to the age of 91, and his help was invaluable in identifying artefacts found in the rubble of the mill. Patrick Chalmers recalls that many of the items sieved out of the fire debris were unrecognisable. *"We used to take them to Sam and he could always tell us what part of the equipment it belonged to. We were able to reuse and refit a lot because of Sam's specialist help."*

Many Stotfold people knew Sam Randall well, especially since he provided lots of advice during the rebuilding process, though Gordon Huckle remembered he did have grave doubts that the Mill would ever run again. *"He would walk round the site in his old mac, with his cap on, hands behind his back and a fag in his mouth and mutter, 'They reckon they'll get it going. They never will'."* On the first day the

Chapter Three

machinery operated again, Gordon dashed round to get Sam and brought him down to watch the Mill working. *"See, Sam, we did it!"*

Freda Stevenson, like many people, remembered Sam as a *"great character with a wicked sense of humour, who always knew all the scandal in the village."* Frank Hyde said, *"Sam was like something out of Dickens. He never used carbons, so as invoices he had long, horizontal printed sheets with separate sections for him, the customer and so on. All were hand written with a scratchy pen which he had to keep dipping into the ink."*

Ron Roper said fondly, *"Sam had a rough exterior but a soft heart. When we didn't have enough money to pay for the slates for the roof of the restored Mill, he paid the £20,000 bill."* Sam Randall never lost his love for the Mill and when flour was produced once again in 2006, he told volunteers, *"I went to bed a happy man that night."*

His contribution to the restoration is recognised in the bronze statue by celebrated sculptor, John Mills, now housed on the Stone Floor. Sam, the last miller, remained a bachelor and a Baptist to the end.

A young Sam Randall on his friend's motorbike, 1932

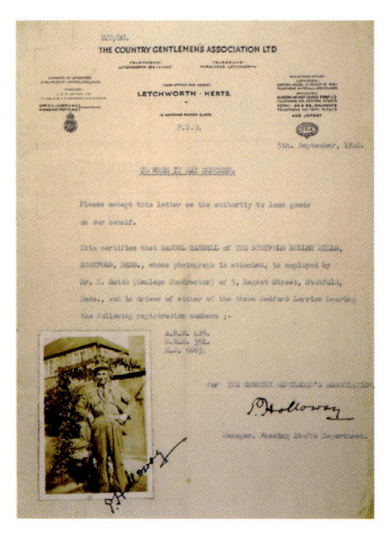

Sam Randall's lorry licence in 1940

CHAPTER FOUR

FIRST HOPES FOR RESTORATION

Though Stotfold Watermill ceased being a working mill in 1966, for many years before that it had only been grinding corn for animal feed. In 1984, Sam Randall reluctantly decided he could no longer make a living from the business and sold it for £186,000. The sale included the Mill, Roller Mill, sheds, Mill House, Mill Cottage and the stables.

There were many rumours about the future of the Mill, including that it might be converted into luxury apartments. Because of the importance of the Mill and its machinery, the Society for the Protection of Ancient Buildings (SPAB) had been keeping an eye on the site through Alan Stoyel and Ron Roper, who was a local SPAB member. Alan, who was then Chair of the Mills Section of SPAB, knew Stotfold

The stone floor before the fire

Chapter Four

Mill reasonably well as he had led a Section tour of the mills in the area on the 10th of May 1980. One of the Randalls had acted as guide to Stotfold Mill and Alan remembered, *"It was wonderful to talk to this old man who knew so much about the place. The millstones weren't grinding flour but everything was running. Our visit was possibly the last time the Mill machinery operated before the fire."*

Stotfold Mill had been granted Grade II listed status by English Heritage on 9th June 1974.

The listing – held on the National Heritage List for England website – entry number 1113870 – gives the background explanation of the criteria, though because listing deals primarily with architectural criteria and is assumed to include fixed machinery, it does not refer in detail to the overshot waterwheel or the Whitmore and Binyon hursting, which a Court judgement of 1987 would state were *'of national importance'*.

The English Heritage listing, based on the entry of 15th August 2013, reads:

'Mill. Early C19 with late C19 additions and alterations. Earlier part has inscribed bricks: "W.P.", "G.Bally 1825", "R.P." and "C.H.". Earlier part has gault brick ground floor and weatherboarding to upper floors. Later parts are of gault brick. Slate roofs. Original block of 3 storeys and attics, later 4-storeyed block to N. Main block: sash windows with glazing bars in moulded surrounds, in asymmetrical arrangement. Plank doors, 2 each to ground and first floors. Sack hoist projects from attic, R of centre. Said to retain overshot wheel and machinery. Late C19 boilerhouse to rear has tall square-section chimney with diamond patterning in red brick. LH block: 3-window range. All sash windows with glazing bars, all under red brick cambered heads.'

With the Grade II listing and with Alan Stoyel speaking in support at the 1986 Local Enquiry, a 1987 County Court judgement stated: *'the work of converting the Mill into a dwelling and a flat was not essential to the proper preservation of the Mill and was not desirable or necessary. Accordingly, the presumption should be in favour of preservation'*. Most significantly, it stated *'the Mill and its machinery are of national importance'*.

When an application for converting the Mill to dwellings came to the County Council in 1995, Alan, on behalf of SPAB Mills Section, again led the objections, concluding forcefully, *'There has been a local initiative to try and save what remains of the Stotfold Mill complex and to bring the waterwheel and machinery back to life. While the possibility exists of such *a scheme coming to fruition no application for the development of the site, or the demolition of any elements should be permitted to go ahead.'*

Ron Roper had completed a six year apprenticeship in electrical and mechanical engineering in London. In 1970 he moved to Luton to work at Vauxhall Motors on pre-production models, then to Kent Water Meters, working in the research division. He stated *"I was always interested in things mechanical but my interest in milling was rekindled on a visit to a windmill in Nottinghamshire near Retford. My uncle had been the miller at North Leverton Mill, but after his death it had fallen into disrepair. I became a member of the Friends of North Leverton Windmill, where I made and fitted new brass bearings for the fan tail and helped with fitting the new sails."*

Ron recalled *"SPAB members were the eyes and ears of the Society and were asked to keep a watch over mills in their home area. This led to my involvement with Bromham Watermill, which had also suffered a fire, on 20th February 1974. A group of artisans had been living in the building since February 1971, earning a living through making pottery and leather goods and it is possible sparks from one of their kilns finally led to the fire. Bedfordshire County Council then took over the building, which had been restored to working order but had no miller so I volunteered to mill once a month on a Sunday and trained two other volunteers.*

Then I decided to make my hobby earn a living and started to search for a mill to achieve this ambition. I was offered several mills, but all expected the mill manager to have a small income from another source, like a pension and would not agree that the mill alone could provide enough support, even though I provided a detailed work plan supported by my own bank".

Ron set out to find a mill he could buy or lease and, after two failed attempts, heard of Stotfold Mill. With his interest in mills and experience in working at Bromham Mill, he was keen to see the buildings restored to working action and spent years trying to persuade the owner to sell or lease the property to him. Stotfold Mill had been on the market for a while, (priced at £250,000) probably since permission for conversion was unlikely, because of the court judgement.

Finally, in 1992, many years of persistent searching seemed to be coming to an end. Ron remembered, *"I came home to lunch on the 15th December at 12.30 and my wife, Lynn, passed me an envelope with a letter from the agent, who had been the go-between in the two long years of negotiations. The letter formally agreed to all the conditions, including a peppercorn rent of £100 per annum, with me*

Chapter Four

being responsible for maintenance and running costs." Ron went back to work, *"like a dog with two tails"*.

At 2 pm – only an hour and a half later – he got a phone call from Lynn saying that the Mill had burned down. Ron was stunned. *"After I heard about the fire, I just felt disbelief and couldn't do anything but sit quietly trying to gather my thoughts. All that hard work had, literally, gone up in smoke. I needed to see the Mill but did this with a lot of trepidation. In fact, I didn't want to go until Lynn persuaded me I had to go and see it. She's a good woman having forced me to take that step".*

Ron first saw the burned-out Mill on the evening of the 15th December at about 7.30. It was dark as there were no street lights near, so he took a torch and also his camera to record what he saw, but since he only had a flash, some of the early pictures are murky. He climbed over the sooty remains of the front wall to rummage through the debris and see what had survived. To his delight the hursting and the waterwheel, because they were iron, were still recognisable and enough of the rest of the nationally-important milling equipment seemed to be intact.

Ron realised that action was needed immediately. *"All the iron parts had had paint and grease burned off and were just bare metal and this was mid-winter. In a few months the lot would have become a rusting hulk and every nut and bolt would need angle grinders to remove them. I bought 20 gallons of agricultural grease and a brush, coated everything with grease and got some canvas tarpaulins from Bromham Mill to cover the machinery. So, everyone else was out Christmas shopping and I was spreading grease."*

As he climbed back from viewing the debris, Ron met Robin and Lorelie Tasker for the first time. Ron said he thought enough of the machinery had survived to

Ron Roper examines the derelict waterwheel

First Hopes For Restoration

An early view of the ruins, with piles of bricks covered in tarpaulins

enable them to restore the Mill. In return, Robin Tasker explained how he had recently been trying to save another Stotfold landmark. A group of people, including both Taskers, had set up a Residents' Association to attempt to prevent the demolition of the old St Mary's School on the corner of Rook Tree Lane, but this had failed and the building had been demolished. Though it was not a listed building, the fight went to a full enquiry and Robin gained a lot of experience that later helped with the fight for the Mill. Robin was a self-employed graphic designer, so was able to provide professional-looking display panels to aid the case and though they lost the school building, were at least able to restrict the number of houses built on the site. He told Ron, *"It is really sad to see Stotfold's heritage slowly disappearing"*. This evening was the start of the two men's determination to join together to prevent the Mill going the same way.

The Ropers and Taskers realised there was a vast amount of work to be done and they would need the help of a lot of people, so they split the work between them. Ron contacted SPAB and influential contacts he had in the area and at County Hall from his Bromham experience. He also talked to John Saunders, then County Councillor for the Stotfold area, who immediately agreed to help. *"Then there were three,"* Ron said.

Chapter Four

John Saunders recalled, *"We soldiered on through some very difficult times wondering how the hell we were going to get on. The one thing we were certain about was that we would make sure the Mill was saved, whatever it took,"* though he admitted, *"When I saw the Mill on the morning after the fire, my heart fell into my boots at the devastation and I wondered if we could really do anything."*

The day after the fire, and following a night without sleep, Robin Tasker began telephoning every organisation he could think of who might help to get the Mill relisted. He carried on throughout the day and also wrote letters to the Planning Department at County Hall, then in Biggleswade, reminding them that the Mill was listed, protected and insured and that he believed it was the obligation of the owner to restore it to the state it was in before the fire.

On 30th December 1992, Alan Stoyel of SPAB Mills Section made a site visit to assess how much had survived, to establish its significance and to ascertain how the important remaining elements of the Mill might be conserved, in as sympathetic a way as possible. The report, completed on 2nd January 1993, initially made gloomy reading, but eventually concluded the prospect was not entirely hopeless:

> *'In strictly architectural terms, this listed building is an almost complete loss. Part of the Mill's importance, however, was as a member of a group of buildings, with watermill, house for steam engine and boiler house still standing and the other structures untouched. Since the ground floor of the watermill has survived, together with the waterwheel, main pit-gear, hurst frame and steam engine drive, much of the cohesion of the mill complex remains, so that each unit of this group of buildings is still vital to the integrity of the whole.*
>
> *The brickwork of the lower part of the mill has survived well, although there is naturally a certain amount of spalling* (Note: spalling is the distortion of brickwork due to the stress of thermal expansion and contraction) *and mortar destruction. The waterwheel, wheel-shaft and pit wheel seem to have been unaffected by the fire, so that the prime power source remains for future use. The cast iron hurst structure has protected the remainder of the pit-gear, and the four spindles with their stone nuts, jacking apparatus, etc. all appear to be in workable condition. The intensity of the fire has charred the upright shaft from top to bottom, as well as the great-spur wheel, but enough remains to be used as patterns in any reconstruction. In addition, the steam engine drive on the ground floor is still intact, only one set of bevelled cogs requiring replacement.*

There are 7 millstones still in place on the hurst, and probably a further 6 that have fallen through the floor. It is estimated that up to 7 of these might be reusable, but it is not possible to be sure until a detailed examination has been carried out following their salvage. Some of the lay shafts and the sack hoist appear to be serviceable from a cursory inspection but careful study of these items is needed to ensure that they have not been too distorted by the heat. The pit wheel cogs have survived the fire and appear not to need replacement, but every other piece of wood in the whole building is destroyed or irreparably damaged. Thus nothing remains of any stone furniture, ancillary machines or equipment, except for odd pieces of ironwork.'

Alan's conclusions and recommendations summarised the Mill's continued importance:

1. *The combination of watermill, steam engine stack and house, roller mill, wagon shed and outbuildings is a rare survival.*

2. *The gear is particularly fine, representing the ultimate phase of traditional water-powered corn milling. The remodelling of the machinery was by the celebrated firm of Whitmore and Binyon.*

3. *The primary machinery is still fairly complete and restorable to working condition.*

4. *The waterwheel is exceptional and in good condition. It is the widest wheel known to survive at a corn mill in England.*

5. *There is a live water supply.'*

He recommended: *'The best way of ensuring a viable future for what remains is to capitalise on the live water supply and have the waterwheel turning again, preferably serving some useful purpose.... It is very much hoped that the charred great spur wheel and the upright shaft, at least, the lower part of it, can be rebuilt using the remains as a pattern, so that millstones can be turned – even if it is only for demonstration purposes.'*

These gave some indication that the long-term aim of restoring the Mill to working order was feasible. In addition, as Ron Roper explained, "*As there was no security on the Stotfold Mill site, I had gained permission from Beds County Council to store some of the smaller pieces of equipment, that would be easy to steal, at Bromham. That is why the smallest pieces survived the fire and could be brought back later.*"

Chapter Four

Ron stated, *"Alan Stoyel's report was also the basis for the English Heritage relisting, not just for the architecture, but the whole site."* He added, *"I think this was probably the first time a roofless building was given listed status, based on the rarity of the machinery, with the inside of the building saving the outside, rather than the other way round as it is usually."*

However, despite the Stoyel report, the future looked bleak, as Frank Hyde related. *"No-one could really imagine that heap of ash would rise again like a phoenix"* and the Stotfold Annual Town Meeting minutes of March 1993 sadly recorded the *"loss of Randall's Mill due to fire."*

Despite the damage, lack of money and lack of helpers, Ron and Robin were determined to press on with attempts to restore the Mill. John Saunders was approached for assistance, because of his experience of working in local government and he negotiated the support of the County Council for the project. John also suggested that a good way to gain local help was to make a formal presentation at the Stotfold Annual Town Meeting

The official minutes of the meeting, held on Wednesday, 18th March 1998, read:

'*GUEST SPEAKER: RON ROPER, STOTFOLD MILL PRESERVATION TRUST*

Mr Robin Tasker gave a brief run down on the history of Stotfold Mill before Mr Roper gave a very informative talk along with the aid of a slide show on the existing condition and future proposals to restore Stotfold Mill. The Mill has been acquired by the Stotfold Mill Preservation Trust who are seeking both financial and manpower assistance in order to bring the Mill back into working order. The Land to the rear of the Mill is to be preserved by the local TEASEL group. It is hoped that part of the Mill could also be made into a Museum, a home for the Local History Group and an Ivel Valley Way Office. Mr Roper asked any willing hands to complete a form for offers of help in any way to aid the restoration of the largest water wheeled Mill in the County.

Recommended *that the Town Council write to*

i) Wiggins PLC, Hallam Land Management and Richard Daniels to request funding by means of planning gains towards the restoration costs of the Stotfold Mill.

ii) Mid Beds District Council to look into whether the funding allocated

First Hopes For Restoration

for Bury Farm buildings could be earmarked for the restoration of Stotfold Mill.

Councillor Mrs Hyde thanked Mr Tasker and Mr Roper for their attendance and presentation and also Councillor Collier for their efforts to achieve the restoration of Stotfold Mill.'

Following this presentation, the support of the Town Council for the project was assured and a small group of people signed up to help with clearing the debris and starting the restoration.

A long period with many letters and meetings followed as efforts were made to secure ownership, until in 1998, the Mill was sold for £1 to the newly-formed Stotfold Mill Preservation Trust. The group was then faced with the formidable task of raising funds, finding volunteers and then organising the restoration of what a local paper had described six years previously as *'a charred wreck'*.

The Ropers and Taskers had decided early on that some preliminary work had to be done; this included covering the Great Spur Wheel and the waterwheel and making a photographic record of the site. Lorelie Tasker said, *"It was such a special building. We thought if it got a high enough profile the restoration would start to take off."*

The immense task facing the volunteers.
(The set of stones at the bottom left would later be fully restored)

Chapter Four

From the start of work on the Mill, Lynn Roper kept a work log detailing the people involved, the work done, the number of hours and even the weather. The first entries recorded the Tasker and Roper families' desperate attempts to preserve and secure the ruins and by the 18th of May 2002, Lynn's calculations show that volunteers had spent a total of 3,608.5 man-hours working on the Mill. The early entries of the log deal with absolute basics like repairing and securing the doors, sorting bricks and repairing the damaged front wall, to prevent vandalism, though it also records the delight of the volunteers who had watched *'the nesting box of a pair of blue tits in a cast iron support and been entertained by the birds' endless task of feeding their young. As the noise & bustle was going on all around, the birds totally ignored these strange creatures at their work.'*

The first group of 13 volunteers, detailed in Lynn's log, besides the Ropers and Taskers, included Phillip, Janine and Trevor Radford, Geraldine and Louden Masterton, Gordon and Frances Huckle and John and Freda Stevenson. Though she was prevented from doing any of the physically-challenging work, because of health problems, Lynn Roper kept everyone's spirits up by making tea *"on a portable gas ring, in an area between the Mill and the Roller Mill, cold and dark, with a corrugated iron roof"* and the Stevensons' dogs – Jack

Ron Roper surveys the wreckage that had collapsed onto the ground floor

and Jill – provided entertainment. The core of thirteen were joined on various occasions by other helpers, but the group was usually about this number, rising only on one occasion to twenty.

Lynn admitted, *"There were times when someone had had enough and wanted to throw in the towel but someone else in the group would be feeling determined that day and over tea a discussion would take place and, boosted by positive talk, hot tea and biscuits, the wavering evaporated and the task in hand was met with greater determination than ever."*

The Radford family had moved to Stotfold from Hatfield in 1997. They first saw the Mill when walking round to explore their new area, saw the plaque about the Mill Preservation Trust, looked over the top of the wall and saw the devastation. They went away thinking, *"It would be nice if it could be rebuilt"*, so when they later attended the Town Meeting and heard about the need for volunteers, they signed up as happy to help. There was a list of jobs from electrics to gardening, but they put themselves down as general labourers, despite the fact that Phillip Radford had trained as an architect and draughtsman and later worked as an executive engineer, installing telephone exchanges. He commented *"I knew nothing about mills before I started, but as an engineer I can turn my hand to almost anything."*

Gerry and Louden Masterton had come to Stotfold in 1964 from St Albans, where Louden had been working as an aerodynamicist at Handley-Page. When Louden got a new job with Hawker-Siddeley in Hatfield, they ended up buying a house in Stotfold. They heard the plea for help with the Mill just as Louden was about to retire and, as he had engineering experience, thought it would be *"good for both of us to get involved"*.

The Huckles are an old Stotfold family; indeed one of Gordon Huckle's ancestors was named as a 'Stotfold rioter' of the early 19th century. Gordon's interest in local history and background in engineering were a significant asset and both he and his wife Frances worked tirelessly on the project. Lynn Roper recalled, *"There was so much camaraderie. Frances worked like a navvy with the wheelbarrow. For a woman she was so strong."*

John and Freda Stevenson lived opposite the Mill in Stotfoldbury and both supported the clearance by lending tools and providing physical assistance. The original group was later joined by others at various times, including Mark Harris, Claude Ingrey, Dorothy Lindsay, Adrian Morrow and Jackie Radford.

Chapter Four

In July 2000, Lynn reported that *"Jean and John from Luton, used fantastic but noisy equipment to remove lime-scale from the waterwheel. This task has proved extremely difficult as the volunteers have only had a hammer and chisel for this job."* They worked a 10-5 day and made excellent progress but Lynn added sadly, *"The job in hand will require further hours work to complete. One eighth of the wheel now descaled."*

Andrew and Joan Lamb, Sarah Martin, Nina James and her brother Peter were other early volunteers. Louden Masterton recalled *"Peter was very good on the engineering side and collaborated with Phil Radford. He was a key volunteer for years, until he moved from Stotfold."* Other early volunteers were Sid Bygrave, Martin Cole, Catherine Dimmock, Emma Lawrence and Roger Vass. The Tasker sons, Julian and Tamlin, also assisted on occasions, as did Wendy and Dave Wheatcroft. Ron Roper's sons, Simon and Kevin and the latter's girlfriend – later wife – Tracy were also persuaded into helping, while Louden Masterton recruited Patrick and Heather Chalmers who had recently moved to the town and joined the Saturday working groups in January 2000 *"as a way to get to know people – and then the Mill took over",* as Patrick ruefully confessed.

Throughout all the stages, the Mill restorers were also lucky in having the memories and advice of Sam Randall, the last operating miller. After he had sold the Mill, Sam had moved into a nearby cottage in Wrayfields and, at first he was very negative. Jane Hyde remembered him saying, *"There's no point in anyone doing anything. Nobody wants to see an old place like this rebuilt."* As he realised the growing momentum of the project his attitude changed and he became really pleased about the restoration effort. However as Louden Masterton recalled, *"Sam and Ron Roper did not always see eye to eye. There were more than occasional disagreements about what was possible and reasonable"* and Gerry Masterton commented, *"Sam used to say 'You don't know what the hell you're doing here' – but he used much more colourful language."*

The commitment of this relatively small number of enthusiastic people meant that, despite the huge amount of work involved, the restoration project could become viable.

CHAPTER FIVE

BLACK AS HELL WE WERE

On a wet Saturday afternoon in 1998, six years after the fire, a small group of volunteers walked through the gate, forced their way through the large tangle of bushes that had taken root, climbed over piles of ash and rubble and reached the remains of the broken and rusting machinery. Years of painstaking and backbreaking work were to follow as these dedicated people brought Stotfold Watermill slowly back to life.

Gerry Masterton recalled looking at the ruined Mill and thinking *"This is ridiculous. We'll never do anything with this. Rubble and ash was a foot deep in places and everything was open to the sky."*

Crown wheels had slipped down the charred shaft

Chapter Five

Trev Radford commented: *"When you walk around this stunning building today, it is difficult to imagine that it once took a considerable amount of time and effort just to climb through the wreckage to get from one end to the other. I well remember the excitement when we finally cleared a path – a foot wide – right down to the far wall, to make it easier to get a wheelbarrow in to clear the vegetation and debris that covered the waterwheel."*

A temporary roof of plastic sheeting enabled the volunteers to clean the main part of the building and then start to clear the engine house. The roof leaked badly and Trev Radford recalled one committee meeting spent dodging drips. He commented, *"We had great fun crawling on that makeshift roof to batten down the plastic."* At the start, the work was salvage, just clearing the debris and since many people were working during the week, their Mill tasks were done from 2 to 5 pm on Saturday afternoons. Over 60 tons of ash and rubble were dug out, by hand, *"like moles"* as Jan Radford commented and every spadeful was painstakingly sieved to ensure that no item that could be used in the restoration or that had historic significance was lost. Frances Huckle remembered Sarah Martin *"working hard with her shovel and chatting to Sam Randall about the pieces we found. She got on well with Sam"*.

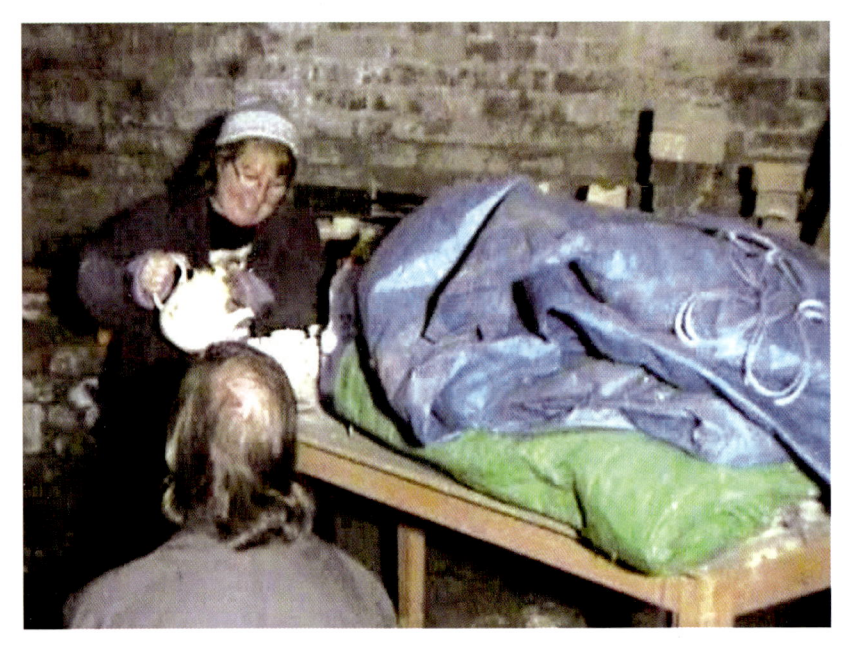

Lynn Roper keeps up volunteers' spirits by making tea in very basic surroundings

Jan Radford added, *"Sam blew hot and cold. One day we were doing a really marvellous job, the next he'd say, 'I don't know why you're bothering'. We never knew what his reaction would be. I think he found it hard to accept we, who knew nothing about it, could get things done."* However, his love for the building was clear and on the day the Mill formally opened, Trev Radford remembered seeing Sam, who had left the official party, affectionately patting the front wall.

All the rubble was piled up in the garden of the Roller Mill, where the volunteers separated out the bricks, in the hope that they could be re-used. They formed a human chain, passing the bricks hand to hand and were instructed by John Hyde in the correct way to stack them. Gerry Masterton recalled *"What a job that was, separating them all out and chipping off the mortar. Then the next Saturday, we'd need to move the bricks to another place. Phil Radford threatened to bring down a pile of bricks and leave them on my doorstep – he knew I hated those bricks so much."*

Peter James also remembered how hard the work was. *"I used to walk the fields and river near the Mill. One day I met Ron and Phil and was asked to come to a Saturday work party to help. I hadn't imagined seeing retired men and women moving great lumps of steel. There was no light work at all; it was all heavy stuff. We had a pulley and that was about it."*

Robin Tasker on the cleared ground floor before rebuilding starts

Chapter Five

Frances Huckle recalled, *"It was a dickens of a mess. We had to clear a track so we could just get to the rubble. It was lovely when we got down to the concrete floor. We were forever sweeping and getting in a bit further each time. We worked our way right through till it was finally clear. Black as hell we were. It was very dangerous, with big holes in the floors and there were so few of us to do such a lot, but we had great fun, clearing all the nettles first and then the buddleia, which was everywhere, on the walls, growing in the wheel buckets. No matter how we thrashed it, it came back. We saved everything we could in case it came in handy later. We even saved the nails, screws and bolts. The intention was to use as much of the original and rebuild it as it was."* She confessed, *"We did think we were being a bit ambitious."*

The volunteers rummaged through the ashes, saving as many of the original bricks as they could. Slowly other items started to emerge, like the millstones and finally the charred main shaft. Frances Huckle said: *"We ladies scratched at it till we got to the oak and then took all the cindering off and rubbed it with wire brushes."*

Louden Masterton recalled *"The shaft was very, very black all round. We originally thought it would rub off and we could re-use it, so various of the ladies, Gerry, Frances and Jan Radford sat around, legs dangling down, wearing overalls, goggles and hats, rubbing furiously away."* Gerry remembered cycling home *"and getting very funny looks*

Gordon Huckle watches the pile of debris being removed

from people as I went along Rook Tree Lane. When I looked in the mirror at home I knew why. My face was black, except where the goggles had been; I looked like a panda, but no-one had mentioned this before I left."

The group also wire-brushed the cast iron columns of the hursting frame and all of the structural steelwork, to remove years of accumulated grime and rust. Despite Ron Roper's efforts immediately after the fire, the long years before restoration could begin had taken a heavy toll. The work continued to be difficult and in some cases quite dangerous. Louden Masterton remembered two occasions when his foot went through the floors, including one incident involving what had been the old Mill toilet facilities, a removable floorboard on the ground floor, which was flushed by the water from the wheel.

As well as the stacks of bricks, the rubble pile continued to grow and as the group had no money they had to work out how to get rid of it – for free. NTL were busy in Stotfold at the time, digging up half the roads to put in cables and everyone was fed up of the annoyance *"There were very bad vibes,"* Louden Masterton said, so he rang NTL, explained what adverse publicity they were getting and suggested that if they moved the rubble they would *"get the reputation of being a smashing firm."* To everyone's delight, NTL agreed and sent a subcontractor with a lorry and grab which made four or five journeys to the landfill site in Arlesey with the 60 tons of rubble. This amount could be exactly verified as it passed over a weighbridge before entering the site. It is particularly impressive to remember that all the rubble and the thousands of bricks had been moved from the site – by hand and wheelbarrow – by a relatively small group of people.

Then they moved on to the machinery. Patrick Chalmers recalled the removal of the huge ironwork pieces being *"incredibly heavy work – we really struggled. Eventually an old block and tackle was found and hitched onto the shaky beams, which meant we could move the cast iron supports and the gears and wheels so they could be cleaned and painted."* The volunteers also gained additional help from Dave Chellew, who lent his lorry with a large grabbing arm, enabling bigger pieces of debris to be moved more easily. *"We bought him a case of beer for lending it,"* Gordon Huckle remembered.

At first there were no doors to make things safe and the site was open to the elements and potential vandalism, so some of the volunteers went to talk to the manager of the builders working at Fairfield Park for Wiggins PLC. He was very helpful and allowed them to salvage some doors, several useful cupboards and fire extinguishers, all of which helped to safeguard the Mill remains. A padlocked sliding door

Chapter Five

from Fairfield was used to close off the entrance to the machinery and Andy Rowell donated tarpaulins, used as drop-down sides for lorries, which meant they could cover the wheel and also could carry on working even if it rained.

As part of their regular schedule, the Ivel Drainage Board had begun to drain the river on both sides of the Mill. The river was dammed and water diverted to the bypass stream. Once the water had been removed, the volunteers could see clearly that the wooden sluice was badly rotten and needed replacing. John Hyde suggested that, as the river was already dammed, it was an ideal time to replace the sluice with new oak timbers, though they would only have ten days, in which to complete the work. Since it was key to have good water and control over it and there was no funding available, John Saunders paid the costs and John Hyde provided the workforce, including carpenters Gerry and Stuart Norman, to install the new sluice. Work started in early 1998 on a wet and misty day and when it was complete, Trevor Radford commented, *"The sluice wood looked so beautiful and new against the charred ruin behind it."* John Dunn then painted the black girders of the sluice gate and the cast-iron beams over the waterwheel, after removing the rust. He remembered, *"It was very cold and cramped as I had to get right to the back, in the small space above the waterwheel"*.

Robin Tasker's letter of 5th July 1999, to Mark Simmons, the County

John Hyde during work on the sluice gates

Planning and Conservation Officer, shows the huge scale of the task, listing nine completed projects: total rebuilding of sluice gates; sorting, cleaning and stacking all bricks; sorting through and removing all ash and plant growth from machine floor; clearing and stacking all loose ironwork; repairing door and window boards and fixing locks; co-operating with River Ivel Drainage Board to restore water way; cleaning the waterwheel and pit and rotating wheel; putting a temporary cover over the hurst and machinery and producing engineering drawings of the great spur wheel.

There were an additional six projects in progress: *'clean, repair and paint hurst and machinery; quotations in hand for rebuilding great spur wheel; Levitt Partnership instructed to draw up plans for rebuild; fundraising now underway; enquiries underway for construction of temporary roof and clearing of rubble from engine house'.*

In 1999 the flagstones on the ground floor were uncovered and volunteers started oiling the moving parts of the Mill machinery in an attempt to get the mechanical gearing freed up. Preparation work began on removing the burned beams which had supported the first floor so John Hyde's building team could start work. Lynn reported with delight on 20th November *'The temporary roof covering is being fitted! At last!'*

The huge amount of work undertaken by this small group of volunteers cannot be underestimated. Just clearing the engine house took them from 22nd January 2000 to the 18th March, but they were already

The Mill decorated with flags for the first Open Day. Note the temporary roof of wood, tarpaulins and corrugated iron, with the old shaft still in place

Chapter Five

looking ahead to their first Open Day on National Mills Weekend, which involved *'descaling the waterwheel, clearing the stream, clearing weeds and mowing the grass in front of the Mill',* plus running stalls to raise funds and awareness. Despite this, Lorelie Tasker commented,*"It was really fun as we had a common objective. However absurd the project sounded, it never occurred to us to give up. Robin believed we were living in Mill House so there had to be a mill. We were both local and had seen the Mill working when we were children and had both fished in the millpond. We were determined to get it working again."*

Another milestone occurred in 2000 when the waterwheel first moved a quarter turn, but problems of unwanted access continued to trouble them, though the work carried on. On 28th July, Lynn's work log noted, *'Repair to damaged lock from vandals. Hard work continues to descale the buckets of the waterwheel. Removal of fire debris from above the pitwheel. Consultation about further security to areas of the Mill building to keep out intruders'.* Finally, in March 2001, a new front door was fitted and security was less of a problem, though access was still possible from the unoccupied Roller Mill site next door.

National Mills Weekend in 2001 was cancelled due to the foot and mouth epidemic, but the Open Day went ahead, before the volunteers once more concentrated on *'general clearing up and making preparations for the 1st of July when John Hyde moves onto the site'.* The shell of the Mill would now be constructed by a professional builder, so for safety reasons volunteers were virtually excluded from the site until February 2002, though they worked in the background, cleaning many of the original, saved bricks for the builders to re-use.

During the restoration, pieces that had originally been part of the Mill continued to be donated, like the two horses, which had been part of the millstone furniture and had been removed before the fire. In addition the volunteers often learned about possible useful sources of materials or equipment. Patrick Chalmers recalled going with John Hyde to John's uncle Frank's barn. *"We picked up these wood-wormed bits of miscellaneous wood that eventually became a grain cleaner"* and also remembered going to an old forge nearby *"to pick up some miscellaneous metal that obviously meant something to somebody."*

The original volunteers formed strong friendships and have fond memories of some of the social activities that helped keep them motivated. Heather Chalmers particularly remembered the first Christmas party for about 30 people. *"It was held in the shell of the Mill in what is now the Tea Room, which had only two pillars holding up the roof and trestle tables. There was no heating or lights, so we had two long extension cables to the next door houses to give lights and to run a hot cupboard for the food."* Her husband Patrick provided the meal and a wonderfully ornate menu card was devised to mark this special occasion.

Restoration work had begun as soon as the worst of the debris was cleared, but the Mill was not finally completed until 2006 after eight years of hard effort, almost all by volunteers. There were moments of doubt, though. Patrick Chalmers confessed, *"Most of us never really thought in our heart of hearts that it would come to anything. We thought we might end up with a wonderful, well-cared-for ruin"* and Gerry Masterton remembered often thinking *"We'll never do this – especially after we visited Redbournbury Mill, when we really saw what we were aiming at"* but she added,*" We did get a lot of fun from it. We were such a good little gang."*

However the tenacity shows through in Lorelie Tasker's words, *"There is an enormous amount you can do if you are determined, that doesn't cost a penny. Robin thought it was really important to use local people, and it was a real bonus that we were all working to a common aim, to preserve the Mill for the future."*

Throughout the restoration process it was vital that the Mill volunteers could communicate with the residents of Stotfold and gain their support. More recently this has become simpler as the monthly town newsletter '*Stotfold News'* contains a regular Mill column, originally written by Trev Radford and now by Pam Manfield. In the early days '*News from the Mill*' came in the form of a mini broadsheet page, also written by Trev Radford and pinned to a notice board on the front wall of the Mill building. He said, *"I had to employ all my powers of blind optimism to persuade people that this heap of ash and rubble could and should be saved. When I read the articles today, with the benefit of hindsight, it's a very curious feeling, because we have achieved far more than we could ever have imagined back then. If nothing else they are a useful contemporary record of our plans and progress but they also remind me that if you don't ask, you don't get and that a great deal can be achieved if you really believe in something."* He continued, *"We asked for the help of the people of Stotfold and we certainly got it."*

During the creation of the Trust and subsequent restoration, Alan Stoyel of the Mills Section of SPAB was kept informed of progress and asked for advice, which he gladly gave. When interviewed in 2012 his comments reflected the amazing achievement of the restoration and the fact that it went much further than just the recreation of a building. *"The whole thing was just brilliant! It is very heartening to see how it brought the village back together and incredible how much funding it attracted. However,"* he added, *"it's a good thing you're not trying to raise those amounts now."*

CHAPTER SIX

REBUILDING TESTED ALL MY SKILLS

John Hyde, a prominent local builder, whose family have lived in the Stotfold area since at least 1760, first worked on the Mill in the 1970s, doing repairs for Sam, George and Ruth Randall.

He recalled how he became involved in the restoration. *"In late 1993/ early 1994 I was negotiating to buy the Roller Mill and, if I had got it, would have become responsible for the derelict Mill as well, but my offer on the Roller Mill was refused. After the formation of the Trust, there were several meetings with the Trustees who wanted to know if I was interested in working on the rebuilding and secondly, if I was able to do it. I had done restoration work in Stotfold, on Gordon Huckle's cottage and on Poplar Farm and had won four civic awards from North Herts District Council and others for restoration projects, but these were not in the same league as the Mill. I took some time to consider as I had previously never reconstructed, as a whole, a Grade II listed, timber-framed building. There were numerous elements that were unique and demanding and posed major headaches."*

Before John began work, there were many pre-contractual preparatory negotiations. One of the most important meetings, held at the old Mid Bedfordshire Council offices in London Road, Biggleswade, included John Hyde; Peter Weston; Mid Beds Planners; the Fire Officer; the Conservation Officer and Robin Tasker. This discussion was critical to decide if the restoration plan was feasible. Without the Fire Officer and Conservation Officer on board and planning approval the project could never have got started. Finally, the general plans were agreed and Peter Weston then provided drawings which were subsequently also approved, after which work could start on the restoration.

The first £20,000 grant from Mid Bedfordshire District Council enabled the Trust to set up procedures to get to the point where the project was viable. Then a £100,000 grant from Shanks enabled the work to start. John Hyde recalled, *"I suggested that I provide a shell – the whole front of the current building, excluding the old engine house and the chimney – and a slate roof and the feather-edged boarding. This did not include flooring or windows."*

He continued, *"Peter Weston, a structural engineer from Knebworth, did a bare bones drawing and my biggest challenge was to source materials, especially timber and tradesmen. I spoke to numerous timber merchants and fortunately found someone sympathetic – Alan Newbury, the Executive Director of Ridgeons of Cambridge. Alan was in charge of all timber imports for the group so I showed him the drawings and then he and I set out to find a company able to provide the right timber. We went to Scotland for two days, flew to Edinburgh and then to James Jones and Son, who owned a sawmill in Kirriemuir, Angus. They eventually supplied all the structural timber, which was Autumn-felled Douglas Fir from the Blair Atholl Estate. I am not certain I could have managed without Alan's experience, but once I knew I could source the timber I then decided to take on the project. I was unable to give a price for the work. How could I do that? I had no idea what it was likely to cost."*

It was important to have Autumn-felled timber for the work on the Mill as the moisture content in timber felled late in the year is at the minimum. In addition, all the timber was boxed-heart cut and so more expensive, but this cut is vital as it gives stability – *"and the timbers have never moved"* as John proudly noted.

John Hyde in front of the huge timbers which would become beams for the Mill

Chapter Six

The rebuilding in full swing. (Top left) Timber floors take shape. (Top right) The roofing of the Tea Room and Ivel Room – the old engine house. (Below) Working on the walls of the Ivel Room. (Bottom) The flag flew throughout rebuilding, here at Christmas

Rebuilding Tested All My Skills

John's main construction team consisted of carpenters Gerry Norman from Bromham – *"an absolute star"* – and his son Stuart and Dean Brazier and his team, from Stotfold, who were the bricklayers.

Many of the bricks used in the rebuild were saved from the fire and cleaned by the volunteers ready for re-use. 80% of all the used bricks are Stotfold Stocks from the now-defunct Stotfold Brickworks at Wrayfields. Though as many bricks as possible were saved from the debris by the Mill volunteers, there were not enough to complete the job. Fortunately, John Hyde was able to buy and then re-use 7,500 Stotfold Stocks after the demolition of a cottage on The Green, adjacent to Manor Farm.

Sam Randall examining some of the new timber beams

With approval from SPAB and the planners, they used the nearest slates to Welsh Blue that they could get and afford – Glendyne Quebec from Canada. The sliding sash windows were made in Fen End by a local joinery firm and were

The Dressing Floor takes shape

Chapter Six

The Topping Out Ceremony with John Hyde on the finished roof

funded by a grant from Motorola. Mills are traditionally painted in light colours as the flour leaches through the boarding and stains dark-coloured paint, so the feather-edge weatherboarding is painted in a cream paint, called Burlesque. Once the weather-boarding was installed, Patrick Chalmers and Phillip Radford painted it. Patrick remembered, *"It took five days and two coats. We worked out we had painted a mile of Russian white wood weather-boarding."*

Part of the rebuild brief was ensuring safe public access. The builders had to prove that people could get in and out of the Mill safely, especially in case of fire, so the stairs have a one-hour protection against fire, as has the lift-shaft. The second contract also included finishing the fitting out: floorboards; the office; putting in all the utilities; the outside decking; plastering walls; paving between the Mill and the house next door – everything except the milling machinery itself.

The weather-vane was chosen as John Hyde had been told by George Randall that he *"always remembered seeing a running red fox on top of the Mill"*. It was the last weathervane made by Ironcrafts, a small manufacturing firm, once based in Stotfold.

The topping out ceremony, which took place on 11th April 2002, included tying a laurel wreath – symbolising eternity – and a witch's broom – to ward off evil spirits – on the roof and raising the Union Flag. (Throughout the rebuilding, a Union Flag from Trev Radford's collection had been flown, as a sign of the volunteers' determination.) Topping out is an ancient traditional ceremony celebrating the completion of the roofing or the placing of the last beam of a timber-framed building. It is supposedly of Scandinavian origin, dating from pagan times, where it was common practice to place a tree on top of a new building to appease tree-dwelling spirits. The tradition migrated to Britain, Germany, Poland and other European countries with early Scandinavian invaders. John recalled, *"Once we had the building roofed I really felt I'd achieved something."*

In May of 2002, during National Mills Weekend, the partly-restored building was opened by Sam Randall, the last miller, and then

Bedfordshire County Council Chairman, John Saunders. The Vicar of St Mary's Church, Stotfold, Reverend Pat Quint conducted a formal blessing:

"Loving God, we thank you for the insight and vision that has surrounded the preservation of Stotfold Mill. We rejoice that this part of our local history is being restored and will be a living heritage for generations to come. We give thanks for all the work already undertaken and pray that, in your strength, the project may be completed for the benefit of the community and to your glory. And may the blessing of God Almighty, Father, Son and Holy Spirit, be upon this Mill and all who continue to work for the completion of the restoration. Amen."

Once the structure was up, the events group started to raise funds for the remainder of the rebuilding. The Trust were happy with the work on the first contract and felt it would be wrong to go elsewhere for the rest of the project, so John Hyde was also awarded the second contract. Work for 2003-4 included the restoration of the chimney and the engine house. The chimney restoration included repointing all of it, removing all spalled brickwork and reheading. The top five feet of the chimney were in poor condition, so were removed and replaced as *"there was no point in restoring the engine house if the brickwork was likely to fall off onto it."* Arlesey White bricks, made by Beart and Company of Arlesey, were used for the top of the chimney.

John Hyde said of his involvement with the project, *"There were initially times when I had reservations about whether I had bitten off more than I could chew, but once I had committed myself and got into it I never ever thought I couldn't do it. I was in it for the long haul."*

He added, *"This has been the most satisfying job I've ever done. When SPAB gave the award to recognise the quality of the work we were only the fifth watermill in the UK to achieve this. Alan Stoyel said, 'You must be the only builder in Great Britain to have built a Grade II listed building'. I do feel proud of it. It tested all the skills I had accumulated over all my working life as a carpenter, joiner and builder. It has been a privilege to have been offered the opportunity to do this. But it was hard. The Mill was my other half for a long time as my wife, Julie, will tell you."*

CHAPTER SEVEN

MACHINERY MAGIC

Whilst helping other volunteers clear the site, Ron Roper and Phil Radford also took on the huge task of planning the restoration of the Mill's machinery. Their engineering skills and knowledge were to play a key part in the years to come. The restoration work, completed largely by volunteers, with some professional aid, took several years, beginning before the building work and continuing long after most of it was complete. The quality and complexity of the restoration and re-creation work earned high praise in many of the subsequent awards given to the Trust, which provide fitting tributes to all those involved.

Work started immediately after the fire, as Ron recognising the potential to save and one day restore the machinery, gave it what rudimentary protection he could, covering the stones and hursting area with tarpaulins, and applying over four gallons of agricultural grease. Without doubt this helped limit further damage, and in some cases would be the difference between items being salvageable or not.

John Dunn, who would work on much of the machinery restoration, approached Ron in 2002 to see if he could be of help and offered to draw the Mill, minus the front wall, showing the Mill's interior. Ron asked instead if he could draw the machinery which he agreed to do, starting with the pit wheel, using a Computer Aided Design system (CAD). Over the next 18 months John drew some 90% of the machinery including the hursting and the old and new upright shafts, producing 35 drawings of A1 size, which now form an invaluable record in the Mill Archive. John's engineering background was ideal for helping with the restoration work. He had started as a toolmaker's apprentice, ending up as Works Director of an automotive firm in Chester, giving him a thorough understanding of engineering processes. Martin Cole, an associate of Ron, had previously drawn plans of the Great Spur Wheel using CAD; these documents were invaluable to Ray Kilby when he built the new wheel, and allowed John to focus on drawing the milling machinery.

The machinery restoration also owed a huge debt to the engineering skills and craftsmanship of Ray Kilby. Over the years he has made the pit and crown wheel teeth; spur wheel; trap doors; the sack hoist pulley system (including the pulley patterns) and mechanism; installed dressing floor belts; helped restore the oat roller; made grain hoppers, chutes, and a tun for the new millstones, as well as adapting and dressing the new stones, and the French Burr stones; made a mill model; installed the winnower; designed and installed safety railings and duckboards. He also made patterns for the line shaft hangers and waterwheel bucket brackets. He commented, *"I also made all the equipment traditionally used by millers including the stone tools and jigs to remake parts of the machinery, usually from wood."*

The Milling Machinery

The millstones are the heart of the mill, and along with all the milling machinery are powered by the waterwheel, via a complex system of cogs and shafts. The stones themselves are turned by the stone nuts, which are rotated by the Great Spur Wheel. The stones, stone nuts, spur wheel and upright shaft all turn on a vertical axis. The spur wheel is mounted on the upright shaft as is the wallower, whose angled teeth engage with those on the pit wheel, transferring movement from one plane to another. The pit wheel rotates on a horizontal axis on the same shaft that runs through the centre of the waterwheel. Thus the horizontal axis of rotation of the waterwheel is transmitted into the vertical axis of rotation of the millstones. This transfer of rotation from one plane to another is considered to be one of man's greatest achievements, and was imperative for mechanisation.

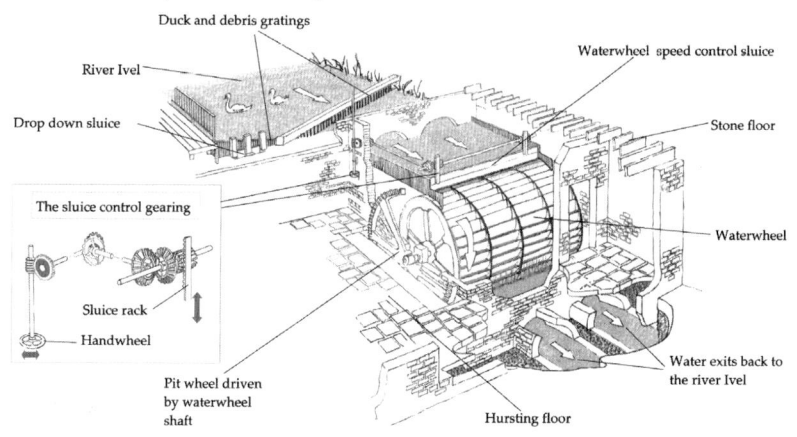

How the waterwheel connects the river to the machinery

Chapter Seven

Ron Roper and Phil Radford inside the wheel, illustrating its scale

The Overshot Waterwheel

Estimated to weigh 5 tons, with a diameter of 8ft (2.4m) and a width of 14ft 6 inches (4.2 m), the overshot waterwheel is believed to be the widest in a corn mill in the United Kingdom and is of great historical interest. Overshot wheels are rarely found outside mountain regions.

John Lampit of Hemel Hempstead, a mathematician and builder, designed the wheel to be self-regulating and as efficient as possible with the shape, size and number of buckets being carefully calculated. Ron Roper recalled being told by Sam Randall that his father, Ebenezer, had watched Lampit over several months, throwing sticks into the river to calculate the average flow of water. Sam recalled, *"Father said this was about 1897-8 and all the locals thought he was mad."* As Ron added, *"No wonder; this would have been some thirty years before AA Milne's Winnie the Pooh made playing Pooh sticks popular."*

The wheel is in four sections, with reverse J-shaped buckets made of wrought iron. Some buckets had to be replaced during the restoration and these are made of Corton steel (as used to build the Angel of the North). Overshot waterwheels are highly efficient, so long as the jet of water is optimised and the wheel is not sitting in the water (this causes drag as the lower half of the wheel is turning upstream, hence is moving against the downstream flow of the water). An overshot wheel turns due to both the power of the water shooting on to its top, and the weight of water in the buckets. The careful design of the buckets and their drain holes ensures as much of the front of the wheel as possible is full of water for as long as possible. The wheel usually turns at 4 to 6 revolutions per minute (rpm) with a very modest flow of water over it, and is self-regulating – if the wheel slows, the buckets fill with more water, so increasing the speed.

During the fire, debris fell on the wheel's heated surface and when the end wall of the building was demolished for safety reasons, further damage was caused to the uppermost buckets. The volunteers tried repairing the distorted buckets with blow lamps and club hammers, but as the buckets are so long, the heat dissipated into what Louden Masterton called *"a heat sink"*. He remembered getting inside the wheel to see what condition it was in and admitted, *"That was quite scary as there was only a tiny amount of headroom inside."*

Prior to restoration the wheel's buckets were full of fire debris; some even had large plants growing in them. Added to this, more than thirty years of disuse, with the hard water of the River Ivel trickling over it, had resulted in half the wheel being caked in limescale, leaving it seriously out of balance and with many of its drain holes blocked. In some areas the limescale was over two inches thick and volunteers would spend nearly ten months chipping off 1.5 tons of it – the equivalent in weight to a family car – using only hammers and chisels as sand blasting had proved unsuitable.

Much of this work was carried out by the wives and sisters of those helping with the heavier restoration work. They took down cushions to kneel on because the edges were sharp and uncomfortable and they went home *"looking like pandas, as we wore goggles over our eyes, but the rest of our faces were black from the soot"* as Geraldine Masterton recalled. Patrick and Heather Chalmers also worked on the de-scaling – *"the most backbreaking work you could ever imagine. We worked with a hammer and chisel, bent over, with our knees resting on the sharp bucket edges beneath, which were digging in all the time"*. Jackie Radford, also a major 'chipper', remembered, *"It was very uncomfortable work and resulted in many unusual bruises."*

Frances Huckle recalled the camaraderie and informality fondly. *"They were happy days. Everyone was so willing to help. We were so free; there was no nonsense about safety helmets at the beginning. We just knelt on old cushions while chipping off the lime-scale. I remember saying if Health and Safety walk in now we'll have to down tools"*. There was

Chapter Seven

Neil Medcalf at work on the waterwheel

no money for insurance so the attitude was *"if we hurt ourselves we accept we volunteered to do this and accept the consequences"*.

The de-scaling was done in stages: one area would be chipped clear, and then the wheel would be turned round a bit further, so the chipping team could clean the next section. Louden remembered with delight, the very first time the wheel turned all the way round. *"Phil and Trev Radford and I were sitting on the sluice beam and pushing hard with our heels. It was quite an achievement; the wheel actually moving round at last."* Trev commented, *"No-one knew what it was going to do because the wheel was so out of balance and the buckets bent. The first couple of times it went three quarters of a turn forwards and then rolled backwards at a horrendous speed and the three of us had to hold our feet in the air to avoid losing them. We must have looked like mad hamsters."*

After more chipping, they managed two revolutions of the wheel, proving it was viable – something which had been in doubt till then. The bearings were cleaned and lubricated, and the inside was cleared out by Louden. Phil Radford, Ron Roper and Pete James fitted temporary weights inside to improve the balance, enough to enable it to turn under water power for the 2001 May Event, after a gap of almost 21 years to the day. John Saunders' staff took the bent and broken teeth and shaft of the gate opening mechanism to a nearby repair shop, heated them and then ran a steam road roller over them to straighten the thick metal.

Once the wheel was cleared of limescale and some repairs had been made to the most seriously distorted buckets, professional millwright Neil Medcalf began work, funded by a Heritage Lottery grant. Neil replaced the wheel's sole plates – the wooden blocks that fit under the bearings to act as a cushion – and fitted new buckets to replace those damaged in the fire or which had become badly rusted. It was not until the 1st May, 2004 that the water wheel was fully restored.

The Pit Wheel and Tank

The axle or central shaft of the waterwheel passes through a brick wall, to link with the pit wheel, at the rear of the hursting area. The pit wheel is made of cast-iron, but has wooden teeth which engage with the metal teeth of the wallower. Everywhere in the Mill, wooden teeth engage with metal ones, rather than metal to metal, to avoid sparks, as flour dust is reportedly forty times more explosive than coal dust and has led to many catastrophic mill fires. The use of wooden teeth also aids quick and easy replacement should a sudden stoppage cause damage, as the wooden teeth break first and can be easily replaced locally, whilst metal teeth are more complex and costly to replace.

The teeth at the top of the pit wheel had been damaged by fire and exposure to weather, but Ron Roper recalled that those on the lower half were found to be in perfect condition as they had been *"pickled in water so much that Pete James and others spent many happy hours with tungsten-tipped drills plus one electric drill (which burned out) trying to remove them. They had swollen with the water and were almost impossible to remove any other way than destroying them."* He added, *"Leaving them was not an option as we thought it better to renew all the teeth at the same time, rather than having part-worn teeth on one section of the wheel."*

The bottom half of the pit wheel sits within a tank in a pit below ground and water level – hence the name. Clearing the tank of most of the water and fire debris was done

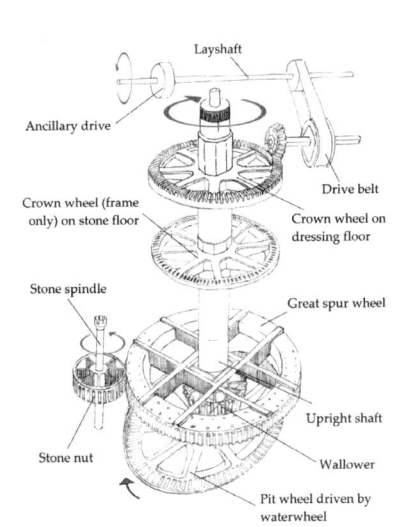

The connections between the shaft and the drive wheels

Chapter Seven

using a very make-shift piece of equipment – a saucepan on a broom handle. However that left the problem of clearing the dregs. Trev Radford was just small and nimble enough to climb down the side of the wheel and into the tank, sitting very uncomfortably on one of the wheel's lower spokes, from where he could scoop up the remnants of the stagnant mud and charcoal, ending up *'very black and smelly'*. The original tank, designed to keep the wheel dry, had been in place since 1897 and it sadly became clear that the passage of time and exposure to the elements had left it badly corroded and leaking. This would cause it to flood, meaning that the new pit wheel teeth would only last about five years and replacing them regularly would be an expensive and time-consuming business. It was obvious the tank would need replacing so local boiler makers, Michael Maskells, were commissioned to build a new one from Corton steel, which should last for 50 years. The new tank was installed by Neil Medcalf with the assistance of John Dunn and Phil Radford.

Phil Radford had been an Executive Engineer with BT prior to retiring, and had also trained as an architect in his earlier years. These skills, along with those he gained in building working miniature steam engines and ships, were all to prove useful time and again throughout the project. Phil remembered the problems involved in dealing with the pit wheel and tank *"To get the old tank out of its position, the pit wheel had first to be split into its two halves. With the hursting in place, the pit wheel could not be lifted out in one piece. The top half was moved into the hursting, leaving room for the bottom half to be rotated around the horizontal waterwheel shaft and then removed, and stored alongside the top half. Each section weighs half a ton. Now the pit tank could be lifted and rotated out from under the waterwheel shaft and up through the hole in the hursting normally occupied by the upright shaft. This operation alone took two days to complete and a reversal of the entire procedure was required to get the new tank into place."*

The pit wheel's 118 replacement teeth, were hand-made by Ray Kilby from oak wood at a cost of £1,100. Ray's involvement with the Mill began after he made replica guns for the Scouts to restage the Royal Navy's famous Field Gun Race at the Stotfold Festival. Ron Roper saw the quality of work involved and said, *"We need the man who made that!"*

Ray remembered his first visit to the Mill. *"The volunteers had just cleared most of the debris away, but the pit wheel was still surrounded by ash. I decided I couldn't do anything useful on site until there was a roof to protect restored items."* So he went home to make the teeth, which sat in store for safe keeping for three years.

Ray comes from a family background of engineers. His father – *"a very clever and creative man"* – was a coach-builder and Ray worked as a design engineer throughout his career. After leaving school he undertook a five year apprenticeship as a pattern-maker for K&L Steel Founders in Letchworth, where he worked from 1966 to 1972. Its output included tank turrets and parts for cranes and steam engines. He then worked at RKB at Sandy for 18 years; this was a non-ferrous foundry, producing intricate castings, including parts for computers. The last thing he made was the pattern for the shield on the front of Virgin trains. He later set up his own pattern and model-making business – Kestrel Design Centre Manufacturing – which made a huge variety of items from 20ft lorry models to calculators, to propellers for a man attempting to cross the English Channel by bike. He patented many items, including size tags for clothes. The company also made the pattern for the radar dome of *HMS Sheffield*, which was lost in the Falklands War. Ray said ruefully, *"I always feel it was my fault it got sunk."*

At the time of writing (2012) Ray remains a Mill stalwart and when on duty at the Mill he is easily recognised by his trademark red neckerchief, waistcoat, bowler hat and (unlit) pipe, echoing the traditional costume of millers of earlier years. He admitted he enjoys both the work on the machinery and the interaction with visitors. *"Perhaps the most interesting for me are the elderly people who remember seeing this Mill or others in operation and are intrigued that the technology is still working today. Visiting the Mill stimulates memories of their childhood, while I find kids today don't really understand the relationship between the past and the future."*

The Wallower

Mounted around the upright shaft, just below the spur wheel, the wallower is an iron gear with 35 metal teeth, angled to engage with the angled teeth of the pit wheel, transferring the plane of movement from the waterwheel and pit wheel's horizontal axle to the vertical upright shaft. It is a single casting, held in place with wooden wedges. The small number of teeth on the wallower, compared to the pit wheel, gears up the speed so that the shaft rotates approximately three times faster than the waterwheel and pit wheel. The wallower is original and only required cleaning to enable it to operate effectively.

The Whitmore and Binyon Hursting

The hursting is the huge cast-iron frame which surrounds the upright shaft and supports the millstones and the associated tentering gear. Made by the firm of Whitmore & Binyon (the Rolls-Royce of mill engineers in the 19th century), Stotfold's hursting is considered to be

Chapter Seven

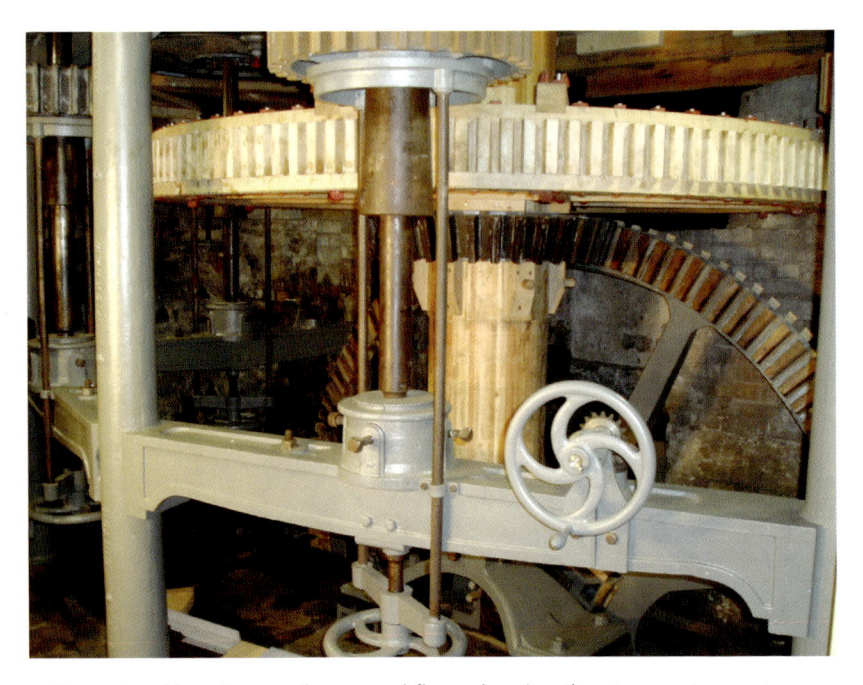

The restored hursting on the ground floor, showing the stone nuts, great spur wheel, wallower, pit wheel and upright shaft

an exceptional example of their work. It was made in several parts to aid transportation; this also meant it could be fitted around the existing shaft and spur wheel. The latter had been replaced after the fire of 1825. The upright shaft shows signs that it may have been installed prior to this date when the wheel was undershot. The original spur wheel had spokes cut into the shaft (compass-arm construction). This made the shaft weaker, but adequate for the lower power of an undershot waterwheel. The present spur wheel is a clasp-arm design, suitable to transmit the higher torque developed by an overshot wheel. The shaft was raised by the lower bearing support casting, possibly in 1897.

Ron Roper explained, *"I think one of the reasons for this was so the weak part of the shaft would no longer be between the great spur wheel and wallower – the area transmitting the greatest torque loading – but also for placing the wallower in the correct position for the pit wheel. We specifically asked for that part of the shaft to be saved, not just because if may be the oldest moving part in the Mill, but so that we can have forensic dendrochronology applied to it, giving us the date the tree was growing."*

He added, *"The great spur wheel does have a mystery. Its nuts and bolts were forged, so they were made before Maudslay invented the screw cutting lathe in 1795. Did they come from the old spur wheel? All we know is that these two items – the shaft and the spur wheel – were already in place when the refit was done by Whitmore and Binyon. That is another reason why the hursting is in two sections so it can bolt round it. So, I think the date order is: upright shaft pre-1825; great spur wheel 1825 and the wallower 1897."*

It is believed that Whitmore & Binyon, based in Wickham Market, near Ipswich and operating between 1780 and 1901, only embossed their name on a handful of their hurstings. Stotfold Mill has one of them, The quality and rarity of the hursting is one reason why the Mill was granted a 1987 court injunction which stated that *'the machinery is of national importance'.*

The hursting is believed to have been bought second-hand (for £433 6s 8d, and may have originally stood in nearby Radwell Mill). The original invitation to tender for the job of refitting the Mill in the late 19th century can be found in the Simmons Collection, ref: 29A7, in the Science Museum in London. The flagstones laid for its installation at Stotfold in 1897 still exist on the ground floor. Because the hursting is of cast iron, it survived the 1992 fire largely undamaged, although as can be seen today the columns on the Stone Floor were slightly warped, evidence of the extraordinary heat generated.

The hursting also includes the tentering gear (used for adjusting the gap between the millstones), and stone jacks used for raising and lowering the stone nuts in order to engage them with the spur wheel. During the restoration it was found that the stone jacks were rusted and seized. Trev Radford recalled *"We tried all sorts of things, ranging from acetylene torches to brute force, to free them up. But we had to be careful not to shear bits off or break parts."*

John Dunn took a leading part in cleaning the hursting, using a very heavy rotating steel brush on a drill and a disc grinder to remove the dirt and rust. Finally, he applied three coats of a special grey paint, recommended by the Society for the Protection of Ancient Buildings (SPAB). He also stripped the levers and pins underneath the hursting and took out the millstone shafts which he machined in Henlow on a very large lathe. John explained, *"It was vital to do this as the bearing was worn and there is no point putting old bearings back."* John said modestly of his role in the restoration, *"It was nice to be involved. I was very lucky to be part of this amazing achievement."*

Chapter Seven

Neil Medcalf, John Dunn and Ray Kilby assembling the great spur wheel

The Great Spur Wheel

The great spur wheel is fitted to the upright shaft above the wallower; its teeth engage with the stone nuts, which in turn revolve the millstones. Sadly, the original wheel, probably dating from the 17th century, was too badly damaged to be re-used, but enough remained to show how it had been built. Ray Kilby took on the task of creating an entirely new wheel – a stunning piece of craftsmanship. The timber was paid for from a legacy from Dalice Noble in memory of her engineer husband, Jerry. Ron Roper recalled, *"A lot of the lifting tackle, winches, jacks, tools, spanners, drills and saws were Jerry's and many are still used in the maintenance of the mill."*

The spur wheel is a large, heavy and complex structure. As mentioned above, it is fitted around the upright shaft, but within the confines of the hursting. Clearly it would be impossible to rebuild it in situ in such a dark and restricted space, let alone rebuild it to the precise specification required. It was, therefore, decided to construct it on the Stone Floor, partially dismantle it and then move it in sections to the hursting area, where the cross-pieces could be fitted to the shaft and the rim sections reaffixed to the cross-pieces.

Before building the new wheel Ray had to carefully calculate the number of teeth it should have and concluded it should be 146. He said, *"I think the original may have had 148 but it would not have run quite so smoothly".* The rim and spacers are of oak, with hornbeam being used for the teeth. A section of the original great spur wheel is on display in the Mill, together with details of the construction of the new wheel. A small sample section of the new wheel is also in the Mill, allowing visitors to see just how precise and heavy the wheel is.

Ray believes his greatest achievement in working on the Mill has been *"seeing how we can recreate a Victorian industry – and it works! My pattern-making teacher used to call us 'surgeons in wood' because of the fine detail of much of the work. When we started recreating the gear wheels, rather than spending huge amounts of money to get the original timbers examined by experts, we just took the advice of a specialist millwright that oak was the best option, with hornbeam for teeth as this has an interlocking, very dense grain".*

The Stone Nuts

The four stone nuts, one for each pair of millstones, are iron gear wheels mounted on a shaft that passes through the floor above the hursting and then through the hole in the centre of the bottom millstone – the bedstone. The upper millstone – the runner – sits on top of the shaft and is turned by it. The bedstone does not move.

A hand wheel operates the jack (or jacking mechanism), which raises or lowers the stone nut on its shaft, thus engaging or disengaging it with the spur wheel. The ratio of teeth between the pit wheel and the stone nuts increases rotation approximately 15 times (the wallower increases it by 3.37, the stone nuts increase the result by a further 4.71), so a waterwheel speed of 4-6 rpm is raised to around 60-90 rpm for the millstones. All four stone nuts survived the fire in good condition and required little restoration, other than cleaning and lubrication.

The Main Shaft

It had been hoped that the original upright shaft – believed to have once been a ship's mast – could be reused, but closer examination revealed that the fire and the subsequent years of exposure to the elements had taken a serious toll. Some sections had rotted to the point where any load on it would probably have twisted it in two, even though other sections were still so solid that attempts to

John Dunn adjusting a shaft

Chapter Seven

Installing of the New Shaft

(Left) The new shaft starts its journey. (Below left) The height of the crane needed to lift the new shaft into the Mill is clear from this view. (Below right) A rare view from the rear, showing the moment the new shaft begins its journey down through the floors of the Mil

Machinery Magic

The successful final installation: (Top) Neil Medcalf guides the crane driver by radio, as the shaft is edged into place. Incredibly, only a tiny adjustment in position was needed. (Bottom) a view of the top of the shaft on the Dressing Floor

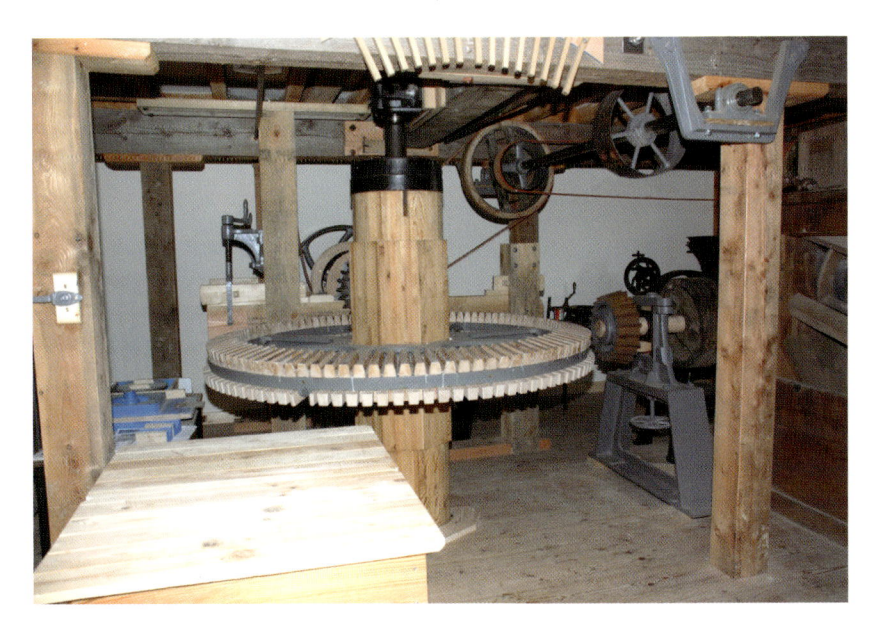

Chapter Seven

bang nails in to it failed.) Gordon Huckle remembered this as the worst moment. *"The main shaft was so terribly scarred. We had been hoping we could use it, but it was so bad we couldn't."* Heather Chalmers recalled working on cleaning the old shaft. *"We were so disappointed about that. We thought we could use it, so we cleaned the charred wood and even gave it a coat of varnish, then we discovered it was rotten and had to be abandoned."* A section of the old shaft is displayed in the Mill.

This discovery left the restorers with a considerable problem as the Mill had been rebuilt with the original 21ft (6.4m) high shaft in place. A new one was required, but no suitable timber could be found in the UK. With the approval of SPAB, a laminated shaft of Siberian larch was made in Denmark, using a construction technique which has been successfully used on Dutch windmills for over 50 years, and also previously used to make masts for large sailing ships like *HMS Victory*. The shaft was then shipped to Boston in Lincolnshire to be machined to roughly the correct size. The great advantage of laminated shafts is that unlike solid green timber it will not warp or split.

Ron Roper recalled, *"The new shaft was delivered to the Mill car park only cut square and was then put on stands and finally cut to shape, mainly round, with some flats to locate the great spur wheel. The original pinions had to be fitted top and bottom with retaining hoops. All of this was done by hand by Neil, standing on top of the shaft and working with an adze."*

Neil Medcalf, who had worked on the waterwheel, also installed the new shaft. Removing the old shaft was easy as it could be cut into sections. Getting the new one in was more of a problem. Various ideas were mooted, such as opening up the front of the Mill, but eventually it was decided to cut holes in the floors and remove a section from the roof. Using a large lorry-mounted crane, the new shaft was lifted and lowered in, with John Hyde sitting on the roof to guide it, until it was gently eased into place on the bottom bearing. The whole job only took half an hour, but cutting all the holes in the floors and roof had taken much longer. This achievement is all the more remarkable as clearance on each side of the shaft is only about two inches (five cm).

The Millstones

There were several millstones in the Mill at the time of the fire; all were damaged to varying degrees by the heat and the years of exposure to the weather which followed, but much depended on their position before the blaze. In some cases, the runner and bed stones had their faces closed together, which protected them from the great heat of the fire and sudden cooling by the fire brigade's hoses. However, those which had their faces exposed were damaged beyond repair. Fortunately, amongst the closed stones was set No.2, a pair of irreplaceable French Burr stones. Ron Roper noted, *"It's possible the Burr stones are over 230 years old as Napoleon stopped the export of these, when we were at war with France."* Britain then had to use alternative stones from Yorkshire or Derbyshire, though these were never as good as the French Burrs.

French Burr, from the Marne Valley in Northern France, is comprised of very hard quartz particles which make it highly valued in milling as it produces very fine flour. Extensive quarrying meant that large pieces of Burr stone became unobtainable, so most Burr millstones are made up from smaller segments of stone, held together with steel bands and backed with Plaster of Paris. The plaster is of a similar weight to the stone – together they weigh 3/4 of a ton. Its use not only helps hold the pieces of stone together but also means only a relatively thin working surface of the precious Burr stone is required.

When the stones are in operation, the bands have to withstand a considerable amount of centrifugal force. It was discovered that the original banding had corroded beyond safe use and the plaster had come away from the stone pieces and was no longer holding them together. Using the original stone crane (part of which was removed prior to the fire and the rest of which had been found in the river by Lorelie Tasker), the runner stone was removed and the bedstone lifted clear of its spindle. Phil Radford cut through the corroded bands, and then he and George Arnold stripped them from the stones, ordering new ones from a specialist company. The damaged plaster was also removed, leaving just the pieces of stone. The first new band, four inches wide, was wound tightly round the stones, cut, and welded into place.

Pete James, George Arnold, Adrian Morrow, Trev Radford and John Dunn then mixed 200 kilos of Plaster of Paris, a layer of which was spread inside the steel band and over the main area of stone, before carefully placing alternate large and small chunks of Burr stone on top. This pudding effect adds strength and makes good use of otherwise waste stone. Another layer of plaster was then smoothed over them, *"like icing on a cake",* then finally the top and bottom bands were fitted. The stone was now lifted back in place and Pete used a laser to check it was level. The traditional method of levelling a bedstone is to use a goose feather mounted on an arm called a hackle bar. Sam Randall referred to this as *a "jack"*; other names include quill stick, jack stick, tram stick and trammel as names of milling equipment often vary from place to place. As the bar is rotated the feather will waggle if it touches a high point. A feather from one of

Chapter Seven

Stripping away the old plaster etc. prior to rebuilding

The new eye of the stone (a recycled sweet tin)

Pouring in the new plaster amongst stone chunks

Trev Radford and Pete James smoothing the plaster. (John Dunn, George Arnold and Phil Radford to the rear)

Machinery Magic

(Above) Phil and Trev Radford, Adi Morrow and John Dunn make finishing touches to the restored stone

(Right) The restored stone on the crane

(Below) Checking the stone level with a goose feather

Chapter Seven

Robin and Lorelie's pet geese was duly acquired and so both modern and old techniques were used to make sure all was level.

Before the restored stones could be used, they needed to be dressed. This is a highly-skilled job, traditionally carried out using hand tools, a skill almost lost today. Phil Radford decided it might be possible to recut the furrows using an angle grinder – which proved to be extremely successful.

John Dunn stripped the slipper bearings of the bedstone and remade them in his home workshop, as well as stripping all seven bolts which adjust the stone position. All were drilled out and re-tapped to put back the threads. This work took several weeks as *"they were terrible to get out"*. John also made a new shaft for the wheel which lifts the stones, reconditioned the cast wrought iron stone crane, and painted it in the same grey as the hursting. He also cleaned the bearings, which are made of phosphor bronze, *"a good bearing material as it resists wear"*. Ron Roper made a replacement screw for part of the tentering gear, the original rusted one having been destroyed during efforts to free it.

Sam Randall was present when the restored millstones ran for the first time and when later asked what he had thought, said, *"I went to bed a happy man."* The restored stones, named Sam in his memory, are now in regular use and produce fine quality flour. This amazing piece of restoration work, led by Phil Radford, was possibly the first time that a French stone rebuild had taken place in the UK for 100 years.

Two other sets of stones were also closed at the time of the fire; these were made of millstone grit, or "Derbyshire gritstone". This can be cut in large pieces, but is a coarse stone, suitable only for grinding animal feed as it wears quickly, leaving a sandy powder in the product. As well as being unpleasant, much like eating sandwiches on a beach, the grit wears down the teeth – not a problem for short-lived animals, but an issue for humans. Indeed it is said that during the French wars when Burr stone was unavailable, British dental health was badly affected, as most people had to put up with grit-filled bread. Charred and cracked gritstones, damaged by the fire, can be seen on the Stone Floor.

Other stones in the Mill at the time of the fire were damaged beyond all hope of repair and had to be lifted out of the Mill by hand for disposal. Trev Radford recalled *"This was something we had to do early on, as part of clearing the site. One stone was leaning at a crazy angle on a pile of debris just in front of the hursting. As we cleared the area, the stone was righted using a hoist from one of the fire damaged beams, and then carefully rolled out of the building. It was very fragile but still very, very heavy. It was another one of those dangerous jobs we had to do. Ron was quite worried, I think, as this thing was heavy enough to cause real damage to us if it fell. Another stone had been in what is now the Miller's Office. If you look carefully, you can just make out its silhouette where the wall around it was blackened by the fire before the floor collapsed and the stone fell down. We actually did not realise it was there until we dug out that area of debris and found it buried."*

Two small used stones were found under what is now the Tea Room floor. Sam Randall explained, *"they were used to break coal on for the steam engine's fire."* A further stone was found buried by the front wall, below the old Mill door, where it can still be seen today. On 12th June 2002, when the volunteers were laying a stone step by the new front door, they found another, very worn, French Burr stone buried beneath the road level. It appears that burying worn out stones enabled heavily loaded carts to stand outside mills for long periods. Ron Roper commented, *"The Mill boundary was 12 feet from the front of the Mill, with the Mill owner responsible for road maintenance. However, it also meant that horses and carts could stand there all day without being moved on."*

French Burr stone is now unobtainable, so when a second pair of millstones was added in 2009, they were a composite stone made in The Netherlands. This 'stone' is made of cement containing quartz grains and is used in many Dutch mills today as a modern alternative. They are reputedly of high quality and largely self-sharpening. This pair of stones – named George in memory of George Randall, Sam's brother – enables the Mill to continue to grind flour even if maintenance work needs to be carried out on the French Burr stones.

Installation and fine-tuning of the new Dutch stones took several months, especially since the furrows had to be reground, but now these stones produce an excellent product. Ray Kilby made a scale model of the runner stone and *"moved the pivot around until it worked"*. Then he and his team did the same with the actual stone – all one ton of it. Ray said, *"I'm not a millwright, but if you don't have confidence in your skills you won't do anything. You just have to want to make things work. We had to take the new stones to bits, refit, recut furrows, level them – and then they worked. If you understand your implements you tend to be able to make a good product. You know their characteristics as you created them."* He continued, *"The composite stones are cast concrete, so the edges rise when they leave the mould and only touch together at the rims."* The milling team had to remove 1/8th of an inch around their circumference to flatten the surface to ensure effective milling. Ray commented, *"They make a hell of a noise when they are not balanced right. It took us some time to work out all the problems."*

Chapter Seven

An historic event occurred on the tenth day of the tenth month of 2010 when for the first time in over a century, two pairs of millstones operated simultaneously at Stotfold Mill. While Ron Roper directed the process and opened the sluice gates, Ray operated the new composite stones, Phil Radford controlled the original French Burr stones and John Dunn carefully watched the grain feed into the stones. Ray commented, *"I was really chuffed to see two stones working as they would have done 150 years ago."* Trev Radford who was also present that day, said, *"I felt more emotional seeing the two sets running together, than I had when we first ran just one, because all of a sudden this was a pukka working mill, not just something limping along on the bare minimum."* As Ron summed up, *"There was the work of many others behind us, enabling us to achieve this fantastic result."*

When the Mill was being restored, phones were put in to enable the millers to communicate between floors, but they soon found these could not be heard when the machinery was running, so came up with the idea of a more traditional bell and rope system. This charming solution works perfectly and, in fact, a visitor remembered that this had been part of the original set up of the Mill.

The Stone Furniture

This is the name given to the mostly wooden pieces of equipment which surround the millstones, including the tun, hopper, horse and

George Arnold turning part of the new horse

Machinery Magic

shoe. These items form a cover over the stones to contain the flour and form a system to feed grain into the stones. It was thought all the wooden stone furniture, except one of the tuns, had been destroyed in the fire, so an entirely new set had to be built for the restored stones. It had been hoped to restore or re-use the one remaining tun, which had been stored off-site, but sadly vandals destroyed it, when they burned down the barn it was kept in, so, photographs had to be used as a guide. Ron Roper added, *"We also visited East Hyde Watermill to examine the stone furniture as this was a working Bedfordshire mill, following the same type of patterns used by the local millwrights in the 17th century."* While the wooden parts had been destroyed, the original small warning bell, which alerts the miller that grain needs replenishing, had also been stored off-site and could be re-used. The fine craftsmanship of the stone furniture was carried out by Phil Radford and George Arnold.

Shortly after completion of the horse, an original that had been removed before the fire and used as a coffee table, was donated to the Trust and returned to the Mill. To everyone's delight the new horse closely matched the original. More surprisingly, at a later date, a second horse that had also been removed from the Mill prior to the fire and also supposedly employed as a coffee table was returned as well. All these can now be seen by visitors to the Stone Floor.

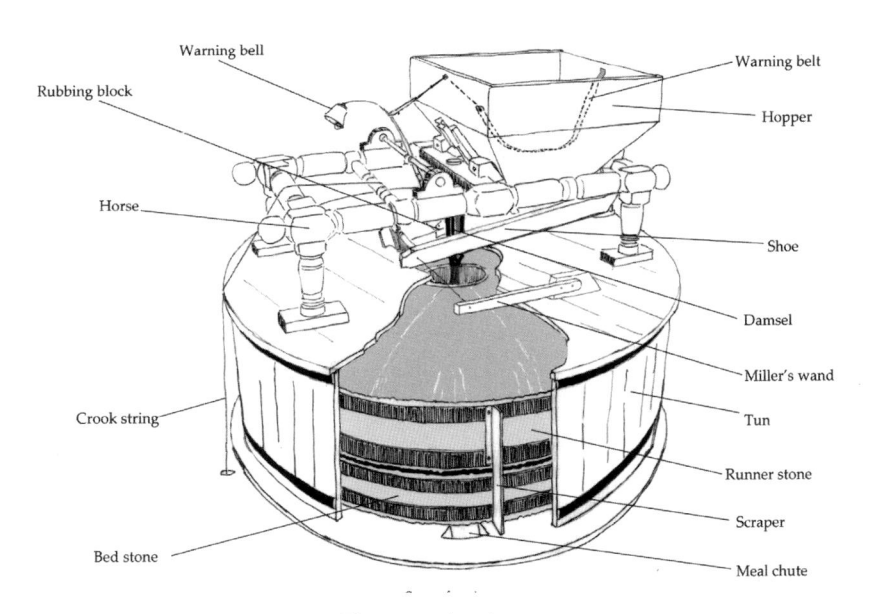

The stone furniture

Chapter Seven

The Crown Wheels

The crown wheels are large, cast-iron wheels, in two parts, fitted with wooden teeth and mounted on the upright shaft. One wheel is used to drive ancillary machinery and the sack hoist and is situated on the Dressing Floor. The second, on the Stone Floor, currently fulfils no role, but would at one time have driven equipment based in that part of the mill. The fire caused both wheels to slip down the upright shaft as their supporting chocks burned away. During the restoration, fractures in the wheels were welded up by a company in Royston, prior to their re-installation by Neil Medcalf. Once again Ray Kilby manufactured the teeth. Ray provides visitors with an easy reminder of the way in which the teeth fit onto various wheels. *"The spur wheel has teeth round its rim, like spurs on boots. The crown wheel has its teeth on top, like a crown."* The bearing diameters on the take-off shaft from the crown wheel were badly worn, but John Dunn found an engineering company in Letchworth with a large enough lathe to machine both bearing diameters in situ, while John manufactured new bronze bearings in his home workshop.

The Diesel Engine

Sam Randall had bought the original diesel engine, made of cast iron from Hollerith (which became ICL). Made by the Crossley Engineering Company of Manchester, it was purchased in 1954 to replace an earlier steam engine for which the engine house and chimney had been built. It was originally installed on a concrete plinth, still in situ, between the Mill and the Roller Mill. The engine was notoriously noisy and was sold in 1966 after the Mill ceased production. Good detective work by John Saunders tracked it down in a local farmyard and in 2008/9 he brought it back on site, where John Dunn cleaned, stripped and repainted it, before erecting it, with Ray Kilby's help. John Dunn explained, *"It was a very complex job that took two and a half months. The most difficult bit was getting the flywheel back on. I had measured the shaft and bore and thought there was plenty of clearance but there wasn't, so there was a lot of heaving and pushing."*

The stationary engine – a 3 horse power Tangy semi-diesel – which is displayed with the diesel engine, was donated in 2011. John Dunn stripped and reconditioned the brass and copper till they gleamed. The engine was probably never used in Stotfold Mill, but demonstrates the kind of machinery which drove a dynamo to generate electricity (where previously millers had used candles or gas lamps) or to drive small farm machinery like corn grinders.

The Dressing Floor

Once the spur wheel was complete and one set of millstones was in place and working, the next task was the Dressing Floor machinery and the sack hoist. Phil Radford visited several mills to research layouts and to see equipment, like bolters, in operation, before he and George Arnold began work on these. Sadly, Phil then suffered a severe stroke. While he was recovering, Ray Kilby got the Dressing Floor machinery into operational order and worked on completion of the sack hoist. Using a complex system of rope, chain, pulleys and belts, the hoist is indispensable for moving heavy sacks of grain and flour into and around the mill. Ray made many of its parts, although the chain and some of the fittings were sourced from Stotfold Engineering who, despite their name, are now based in Biggleswade. Phil had gathered together many of the remaining fragments of the hoist system from pieces recovered from the fire debris and arranged the repair of a large iron wheel that forms part of it, but since no-one other than Sam had seen this in operation, the arrangement of the pulleys and woodwork were based on guesswork and needed trial and error to finally get them working successfully. Of this complex job, Ray's modest comment was, *"It was something of a jigsaw puzzle, but good fun."*

John Dunn reconditioned the bearing housings used on the line shafting, while Phil Radford sourced new double row ball bearings. The housings date from around the 1920s and had felt seals, which were no longer available in the UK, but Phil discovered that a Belgian firm was able to provide them. John and Phil then installed the line shafting.

John added, *"Both the spigot on top of the main shaft and its mating phosphor bronze bearing were so badly worn, that when the shaft turned the whole building rattled and shook."* To stop this, he filed the top spigot round and checked it with a ring gauge. He then manufactured a sleeve, as a press fit to the spigot. The old bronze bearing and its housing were removed and replaced by a double row spherical roller bearings, sourced from Biggleswade.

The restored oat roller

The oat roller, was generously donated by Hyde Mill near Luton, though when it arrived it was unclear whether it could be made operational. Trev Radford recalled the day it arrived. *"It nearly killed us shifting it. We got as many people around it as we could but it still seemed to weigh a ton."* The oat roller was reconditioned by John Dunn, with new bearings and a new bearing block and shafts, as well as some additional turning work carried out in Biggleswade and a new hopper sourced from the former Ironcrafts factory in Stotfold. The machine was then repainted in dark green, with the final detail of the delicate red tracery lines and manufacturer's names and references being added by Trev Radford. He commented, *"This last task involved some very uncomfortable hours lying on the floor to complete the painting."*

A hand-powered chaff cutter was also donated to the Mill. A gruesome machine with teeth to pull the chaff through and two large blades to cut it, this too was restored by John, with Trev again completing the fine detail of the paintwork. This machine is always secured by a protective belt, as it could easily cause serious injury such as a crushed hand or amputated fingers, and indeed a severed hand lies on the floor beneath it, demonstrating the possible dangers. When trodden on, the fake hand moves, which causes squeals of delight from younger visitors as it heads across the room.

Like most of the people involved in the complex work on the machinery from the start, John Dunn is still very much in action at the Mill. He said, *"I enjoy both the people I work with and the visitors. It was great the first time we produced flour and when the new shaft went in, and the first time we had two stones running. There have been so many good points about being involved here."*

The Bolter and Grain Cleaner

Two of the main features of the Dressing Floor are the bolter – a sieving machine that separates the wholemeal flour produced by the millstones into white flour and bran – and a grain cleaner. Both of these rare and historic machines were donated to the mill. The bolter was manufactured in nearby Biggleswade and is in regular use today; the only main item of repair or replacement needed being the mesh that sieves the flour. Jan and Phil Radford were responsible for sourcing this material and Jan remembers well running it through her sewing machine. She explained, *"The fabric has to be stretched around an internal wooden frame and drawn tight by means of a cord passed through a row of eyelets on each edge. It always reminds me of lacing a very stout Victorian lady into her stays, as the cord must be pulled as tightly as possible to stop the flour escaping."*

Machinery Magic

The completed bolter at work

The bolter had an interesting journey into the mill, being hoisted in an almost complete state up to the Dressing Floor by way of the lift shaft, before the installation of the lift cage. The grain cleaner on display on the Dressing Floor is not in use, as a second example, also donated, and installed on the Secret Floor above is used to clean incoming grain. Because of their size, both grain cleaning machines had to be partially disassembled to get them up to their respective floors.

The Dressing Floor also houses a Clean Room where in hygienic conditions flour, bran and oats are weighed and bagged ready for sale – another necessary feature for returning the Mill to production. Tania Beale, along with Jan and Phil Radford, has taken on the important task of weighing, bagging and labelling the various products produced by the Mill – wholemeal and white flour, bran and porridge oats.

The Bin Floor, known at Stotfold Mill as the Secret Floor

The Secret Floor is so called because it has no windows, so from the exterior no-one would know it exists. More properly known as the Bin Floor, it posed many questions about how it could be used. Originally this floor would have housed tons of grain stored in silos prior to milling. Clearly the restored Mill would not need to store such large quantities of grain, so potential uses for the space had to be considered. Trev Radford recalls, *"the suggestions ranged from a small cinema, screening films about the mill, to mere storage."* In the end, the extremely low beams dictated that public access to this floor was not viable; as it is Mill staff have hard hats to wear whilst on the Secret Floor to prevent them banging their heads. Eventually the

Chapter Seven

Secret Floor became a multipurpose space containing general storage; a grain hopper; storerooms for the Kingfisher Shop and Randalls Tea Room, as well as work spaces for the Milling and Maintenance Team; the Archive Team; a hopper for feeding milled flour in to the bolter; a grain cleaner and elements of the sack hoist system.

One of the biggest pieces of machinery on this floor is a large iron wheel upon which a belt is tightened or slackened to engage or disengage the sack hoist. The wheel is original and miraculously survived the fire – and its long fall to the ground floor as the building collapsed – almost undamaged. However four sections of its rim and one of the spokes were missing and without a complete rim the belt would quickly wear or slip off. After some research Phil Radford identified a firm in the East Midlands (Cast Iron Welding Repairs of Coalville in Leicestershire) which might be able to repair the damage, and so the extremely heavy wheel was manhandled into the back of Phil's car for the journey north. Once there, an expert took a small sample of the wheel for analysis as they had to establish exactly what composition the metal was, in order to assess whether it would tolerate being heated to the extremely high temperature required to fuse new rim sections and a new spoke into place. Phil said, *"The firm usually deals with high tech parts for cruise ships, warships and the nuclear industry, so it must have been a somewhat intriguing experience to find themselves involved in restoring a piece of Victorian milling machinery of 'national importance'."*

Although major restoration is now all but complete, the Mill still benefits from the skill and craftsmanship of its volunteers, who lovingly maintain the various pieces of machinery.

CHAPTER EIGHT

STOTFOLD MILL PRESERVATION TRUST AND GRANT APPLICATIONS

No major restoration or rebuilding would have been possible without the formation of the Stotfold Mill Preservation Consortium, which set out to prepare a business plan and gain funding. During the negotiations involved in becoming a charity, in 1995 the official name was changed to the Stotfold Mill Preservation Trust. Brian Collier, who did much of the work for this, commented, *"It was extremely complicated and seemed to take a very long time, but we finally got our charity registration."*

The original plan, as set out in the formal 'Proposal', was to *'restore the watermill to a fully working museum, showing the process and history of corn milling through the ages, using the priceless historical machinery incorporated within the mill.'* The museum would include a gift shop and tea room, with areas where local groups could hold lectures, meetings, concerts and exhibitions. The Roller Mill was to be converted into an art studio and gallery with *'living accommodation for the resident artist'*. Richard Smith, a Bedfordshire-born wildlife artist, is named in the Proposal as being interested in using the Roller Mill as a base for his work.

The wagon sheds were to be restored *'and used to house a museum of steam traction engines and bygones from the Bedfordshire Steam Preservation Group'*, while *'the land running between the river and the run-off stream will be planted and managed as a valuable wild life habitat for educational use'*.

Most of these original plans have now been been achieved, though the group was unable to raise sufficient funds to obtain the Roller Mill, which was sold as a private dwelling. Frances Huckle recalled, "We should have bought the Roller Mill as well but it would have cost an extra £200,000. I said why don't we all put a bit of money in and hope for the best."

Once the newly-formed Trust gained ownership of the Mill, they were then faced with the immense responsibility and costs of restoring the

Chapter Eight

fire-damaged building. The first Trustees were Robin and Lorelie Tasker, who were joined by Brian Collier and Jane Hyde, both members of Stotfold Town Council and by John Saunders, then a member of Mid Bedfordshire County Council.

John Saunders recalled, *"My first connection with the Mill was going there with my father to collect flour for the batter for his fish and chip business. When I was 15 and apprenticed at Gates of Baldock, agricultural agents in the area, I remember Sam and George Randall bought two new Ford 5000 tractors, which I later serviced and repaired, so I've always had an interest in the place."* John has been Chair of the Board of Trustees for many years and said, *"For me, the key points were buying the mill for £1; the first time the wheel turned on its own – and the first steam fair. That proved we could make money to build things to where they are today."* He added, *"In the beginning I didn't see how strong a community spirit we would generate – or what commitment from our volunteers. One Christmas Eve I found Ray Kilby's car standing outside the Mill. He said, 'I woke up last night about 3 am, thinking how do I make this piece of machinery work, suddenly got the idea and came down to look and thought that's how to do it.' That's the level of support we get."*

Jane Hyde commented, *"I agreed to join the Trustees, even though as a churchwarden and Town Councillor, as well as having a family, I didn't really have enough time to devote to it, but I was happy to help get things moving. Until you test the waters you don't know what will materialise. Since they could only have a set number of Trustees I moved aside later in favour of Ron Roper, who was so actively involved in the project."* She added, *"The whole project pulled the community together. The Carnival Committee had died about the same time and people said there was no community spirit and then this community action moved to the Mill."*

To show its support for the project, Mid Bedfordshire District Council awarded the Trust £20,000 as a start up grant. To ensure the money was spent appropriately, the Council asked to have a representative appointed to the Board of Trustees. Councillor John Street, then Vice-Chair of the Planning Committee, was selected and has remained as a Trustee since that time.

As the volunteers started thinking about funding, Robin Tasker was becoming ill, so Louden Masterton and Robin collaborated on fundraising. They went to Mid Beds District Council for advice on how to proceed and met Sandra Einon who recommended they apply for landfill tax money from, as Louden put it, *"the hole in the ground at Arlesey".* This had a further spin-off; because once they had gained landfill money this provided evidence to the lottery that they were a viable proposition.

The first Annual General Meeting of 25th July 2000 listed the names above, with John Saunders as Chairman; Brian Collier as Treasurer; Robin Tasker, Secretary and with Councillor John Street included as 'Mid Beds District Council representative'. As John Street commented, *"Everyone rolled their sleeves up and can be really proud of themselves that they persevered in the early days, as the whole project could easily have been lost. What has been achieved should not be underestimated; this was a huge task."*

A Management Committee was also listed, consisting of Ron Roper (Chair and Technical Director); Louden Masterton (Secretary, Main Fundraising); Gordon Huckle (Main Fundraising); Phillip Radford (Project Leader); Janine Radford (Local Fundraising) and Trevor Radford (PR and Publicity). Sam Randall was included as 'the Miller.'

The Chair's report stated that he was *'delighted to find so much enthusiasm for the Mill's regeneration, locally and further afield, evidenced especially by the very successful Open Days in May which had been attended by around 700 people and had raised about £900 for Mill funds'*. He thanked, *'the dedicated team of volunteers who had already achieved so much in clearing around 60 tons of debris from the site. There was still a long way to go but fundraising was well underway. Application had been made for a landfill grant, which, if our bid was successful, would go most of the way to funding restoring the structure.'*

The first support grants mentioned in the AGM of 2000 were from Stotfold Town Council; South East Beds Community Forum; the River Ivel Drainage Board and Stotfold Carnival Committee. Significant individual donations were also received, including one from Freda Stevenson, who had lived in Stotfoldbury (opposite the Mill) and £30,000 from Dalice Noble (whose late husband had worked on the restoration), which later funded the re-creation of the great spur wheel.

Landfill tax money from EB Bedfordshire was awarded in 2000 and this £100,000 was used to pay for the first phase of the rebuilding work. The Vauxhall Griffin award of 2001 also included funding of £4,000 towards the restoration work. Louden Masterton, who had completed the application went, with Gordon Huckle, to the award presentation in the Social Club of the Vauxhall Plant at Luton.

South East Beds Community Forum gave a number of grants, starting with £425 in 1999, increasing to £500 for *'rebuilding'* in 2002 and £700 *'towards fitting and installing three windows'* in 2004. From the beginning, Stotfold Carnival Association supported the Mill's fundraising efforts, providing £1,100 in 2000, £2,000 in 2001 and £300 in

Chapter Eight

2002. More landfill funds came from Shanks First in 2002. This provided £50,000, which was used for the second phase of the rebuilding. Also in 2002 when Motorola's business in Stotfold finally closed down, they awarded the Mill £12,709.62, from the sale of the site, which was used to finish installing windows in the newly-built structure.

The AGM of 2003 referred to the bid for a Main Grant from the Heritage Lottery Fund, which had been refused as the Mill was regarded as a 're-creation' and not a 'restoration'. It was recommended that they reapply to the 'Your Heritage' sector which funded 'heritage-rich items' and which eventually awarded £49,500 in 2004. A firm in Henlow was paid to develop a presentation pack for the second, successful application. This funding was used for work on restoring the waterwheel and main shaft, as well as interpretation panels about the machinery. These were designed by Calvin Parsons, who spent much time working out how to prevent the panels suffering from damp.

2004 saw the award of another £100,000 from GrantScape which provided funding for the internal building work to be completed. A WREN landfill grant of £26,250 awarded in 2006 paid for the restoration of the equipment on the Dressing Floor and a projector, screen and stand. The 11% contribution needed for this application came from a £27,000 legacy from the estate of Malvene Randall, who

Trustees in 2004, with representatives of the Heritage Lottery Fund (HLF). L to R: Trev Radford, John Hyde, Ron Roper, HLF, John Saunders, HLF, Louden Masterton, John Street, Brian Collier, Phil Radford, Christine Smith, Robin Tasker, Lorelie Tasker

had been George Randall's wife. Paul Redwood commented, "*It is a nice touch that money from a Randall enabled the last major part of the Mill to be completed.*"

£33,001.58 of Section 106 funding – compensation money from developers to the community for the building of houses in Mill View – enabled significant improvements to be made in the Mill Meadows, which were in the process of being transformed into a wildlife-friendly habitat and a recreational resource for the town.

Funding had been acquired to finish off the building, but other objectives were becoming more important. Paul Martin, a senior manager with a national bank, had moved to Stotfold a month before the Mill burned down and later met John Hyde, who encouraged him to become involved in the Mill project. Paul stated, "*It had been an excellent renovation project undertaken by brilliant engineers and builders, but it was clear that business skills were needed to sustain the Mill and take it to the next stage, so it was not just renovated and then left as an empty building*".

In February 2005, Paul Martin was invited to present his ideas about sustainability to the Trustees, as they were aware the Mill needed to be set up as a business to earn money to cover overheads. Someone needed to evaluate objectives and timescales and establish what could be achieved. Paul decided "*to get involved to ensure it was a living building and part of the community, with the priority to get local people in as visitors and helpers. One of the key decisions which aided this was to have a tea room.*"

He presented his full proposals on 7th May 2005 – a carefully worked out strategy to involve as many local people as possible. A public meeting, including brainstorming sessions, was held on the 12th of September in the Simpson Centre and this established the fundraising objectives of the Trust. By 2006 the building was complete and the majority of the machinery was in working order. Paul's proposals made it clear that "*Milling was the first priority, followed by establishing a gift shop, the tea room, an education programme, increasing tourism and raising funds. There were months of indecision about whether we should charge for entry, but we eventually decided this would prevent local people coming back regularly.*"

Paul finally left in 2006, once he felt his consultancy work had been achieved. "*I tried to take everyone's views on board and then got a consensus. I feel you need to understand what motivates people and give them the freedom to go off and do it, but with clear goals. I left when I could see that groups had been set up and were going well on their own. I have learned that you get more out of people if they*

Chapter Eight

make their own decisions, based on clear objectives. You have to let volunteers own what they do. I was very pleased at how things were working and had no qualms about leaving the volunteers to carry on. My reward was seeing how well it was working."

Paul Redwood became a Trustee and acted as Company Secretary for the Board of Trustees from January 2005 until August 2010 and was vital in achieving stability and sustainability for the Mill. He had first became interested in the Mill after he had attended an Annual General Meeting and Open Evening in about 2002. Paul had previously helped set up a national charity Association of Young People with ME (AYME), of which he had become a founding Trustee. There he had learned how to write Memoranda of Understanding and Articles of Association, both essential for the proper running of a charity. He remained a Trustee with AYME for 9 years. In addition, to working in sales for Fujitsu, he had had a broad business background through other posts in the company. After the Mill Meeting, at which he had asked several financial questions, he had been approached to see if he was interested in becoming a Trustee, as they needed someone to help run the Mill effectively. At that time he had refused as he was involved in a high-pressure job and was still heavily involved with AYME.

In January 2005 when he was forced to retire because of severe back problems, he was approached again. Paul stated, *"I discovered that they really needed someone to act as Company Secretary"*. Robin Tasker who had been performing this role had become extremely ill (he died in December 2009) so John Hyde who knew Robin well, arranged a meeting between himself, Robin and Paul, to discuss how to take the Mill forward. Paul recalled, *"Robin was all about trust. If he trusted you, all was fine"* and at the meeting the two men discovered they had a lot in common: Robin was a twin and Paul had twin daughters and they had a common interest in ME.

Following the discussions, Paul agreed to take on the role of Trustee and Company Secretary, if Robin was prepared to hand over responsibility. This was agreed so Paul took away *"about four feet of paperwork"* from Robin, later adding files from Ron Roper, Louden Masterton and Brian Collier. Paul, together with Christine Smith, spent many months sorting out the papers to form a coherent filing system. Apart from organising all this information, Paul saw his first task was *"to bring together a disparate group of people and trouble-shoot problems"*. His experience with AYME was valuable background for realising what needed to be done and his input over his six years at the Mill was vital to ensure the financial and organisational stability needed to take the project forward. Paul commented *"There are so many things I am proud of during my association with the Mill –*

initially sorting out all the problems of which there were many complex ones, managing the Trust during those years – and creating the teams that could (and hopefully will) take the Mill forward. I'm also delighted we gained the Queen's Award".

Although worsening health meant Paul was unable to carry on as Company Secretary – a post which was filled by Tom Ray in 2011 – he continued as a member of the informal TEASEL Steering Group, which amongst other responsibilities manages the Nature Reserve. After the Mill Meadows gained Local Nature Reserve Status, he also became Chair of the newly-formed Nature Reserve Management Committee.

The Mill's official motto, formally adopted in 2009, is 'Keeping the wheels of history turning through the power of volunteers'. Louden Masterton had decided in the early days of fundraising that a slogan would help, so various suggestions were made. The winning idea came from Jan Radford, with the phrase emphasising the importance of volunteers to the future of the Mill being added later.

Several of the founding Trustees were still members of the Board in 2012, including John Saunders and John Street. The other Trustees were Kevin Balderstone, (IT and Major Events Chair); Pat Clarey (Education and Guides) ; Chris Foskett (Treasurer) ; John Hyde (Building Maintenance); Ray Kilby (Milling) ; Phillip Radford (Milling and Maintenance) and Christine Smith (Marketing and Publicity). Chris Foskett stepped down in early 2012 as Treasurer, a post which Tom Ray also took over.

Trustees in 2013. L to R: Phil Radford, Kevin Balderstone, Ray Kilby, Pat Clarey, Tom Ray, John Street, Christine Smith, John Saunders

CHAPTER NINE

STOTFOLD WATERMILL LOCAL NATURE RESERVE AND TEASEL

Almost from the very beginning, the restoration of the watermill and the creation of a nature reserve in the Mill Meadows went hand in hand. Nancy Dawson, a local naturalist, had conducted a plant survey of the Meadows and suggested acquiring the land to lease as a nature reserve, as it was felt important not only to have an industrial element to the mill project, but also a wildlife habitat.

As a result of this, one of the two formal aims of the Stotfold Mill Preservation Trust was to create a nature reserve in the eight and a half acres of meadows adjoining Stotfold Watermill. Over the years these have been transformed by the vision and hard work of the conservation volunteers of Teasel – ThE Astwick and Stotfold Environmental Link. In 2012 the expanded name was changed to the simpler Teasel Conservation Volunteers, as the name Teasel is now well-recognised in the community

In 1993, Stotfold Town Councillor Jane Hyde set up a meeting to introduce the concept of a Parish Paths Partnership (P3) for Stotfold and Astwick. This group of volunteers worked to identify and maintain the footpaths and bridleways around the town and organised regular walks to encourage knowledge and use of the paths. The Midsummer Meander, led by Louden Masterton, has become a favourite element of Stotfold Fête, now Stotfold Festival, and there is still a popular Boxing Day walk organised by Teasel. The footpath group was initially run by the Ivel Valley Conservation Volunteers (IVCV) led by Joel Carré, but rapidly expanded their work and, in 1997, became a separate local conservation group under the name of Teasel.

Mike Thomas who confessed he had *"been interested in nature all my life"* had run nature conservation groups with the British Trust for Conservation Volunteers (BTCV) since 1976 mainly in Bristol, Reading and Stevenage. He then became chair of the South East Region of BTCV, in charge of organising a thousand volunteers on various conservation projects throughout the area. He moved to Stotfold in 1984 because of his job as a chemist with the Furniture Research Association, though he soon moved into a new career as an Environmental Consultant and became deeply involved with Teasel's work.

Once the specialist builders had begun work on the Mill, Mike, Louden Masterton, Patrick Chalmers and others of the volunteers who had worked on the Mill clearance, formed the nucleus of the new conservation group, with an emphasis on creating a nature reserve in the Mill Meadows.

It is difficult today to realise how large a task the volunteers were again taking on. Louden and Gerry Masterton remembered walking near the Baldock Road bridge in 1964 and looking down into what became the Reserve. *"It was a marsh with cows up to their knees in water – a real wet wilderness with cattle, more water than grass,"* Gerry said. The first meadow, furthest from the river was covered with ragwort, which Louden recalled Lorelie Tasker in particular spent hours pulling up. Other problems have been infestations of nettles, dock and great willow-herb which spread rapidly in the damp soil. The typha reeds also demand constant work – *"a rather strenuous task"* as Louden commented in a typical understatement.

Though the lease agreement with the County Council had not been signed, there appeared to be no opposition to work starting. The

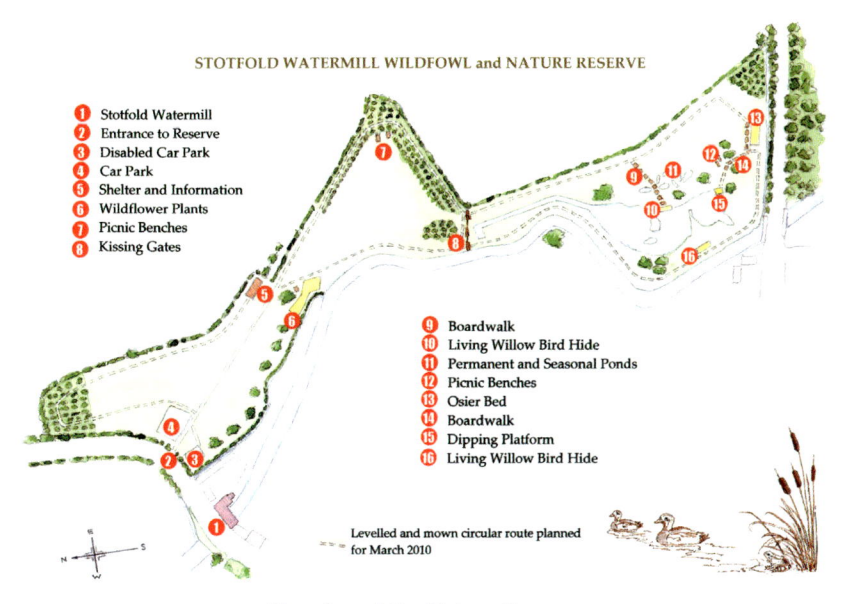

The plan of the Nature Reserve

Chapter Nine

volunteers continued clearing vegetation and moved on to planting trees and hedges, as well as managing Meadow One as a hay meadow. Mike said, "*It took an age to sort the lease and it was a really lengthy process, but we finally got there.*" The initial lease was for ten years, though this was later extended to 25 years – the maximum Central Bedfordshire Council would allow. Paul Redwood who worked on the extension of the lease commented, "*It took over four years to negotiate the extension, and the assistance of Councillor John Street was extremely helpful to the process.*"

The volunteers were always ready to improvise and gain help wherever they could. Louden remembered, "*The Ivel Drainage Board were dredging silt from the river, one afternoon, so Robin Tasker asked if they could also dig some ponds in the meadows, which they agreed to do.*" However, things did not always go smoothly. When the first large pond was dug, the sludge was spread thickly on the nearby field; in February 1999, two schoolboys got stuck in this muddy debris and had to be rescued. A feeder stream runs to the ponds and then back into the river in Meadow Three and keeps the water moving, via pipes buried in the earth at the top and bottom of the ponds. Louden recalled "*At the beginning this went well and then one day the water suddenly stopped. On investigation, we discovered a duck had got stuck in the pipe; it took us ages to get this poor creature out.*"

Valerie Balderstone, who has been a member of Teasel from its early

Bare banks after dredging work on the water channels

Stotfold Watermill Local Nature Reserve And Teasel

Early volunteers at a lunch break. Note the lack of vegetation, trees and hedges around them. The group includes Frances Huckle, Clare Whitty, Geraldine Masterton, Michael Bray, Louden Masterton, Ian Fisher, Valerie Balderstone, Heather and Patrick Chalmers

days, said, *"I've always been interested in wildlife and conservation, so when I saw a local ad about the new conservation group, I decided to join. I'd never been to the Mill Meadows before. Horses had been grazing there and had eaten all the grass but left huge patches of nettles everywhere. For our first work session, Mike Thomas directed us to choose our own patch of nettles and dig it up."*

She added, *"I'm really proud of the first batch of sponsored trees we managed to gain after Mike Thomas left. I was the unofficial tree person and ordered all the trees and tree guards. We had a table at the May Fair and an article in the local papers asking people to sponsor a tree, with rough plans of the layout. We got enough funding for 170 trees, which Teasel and many local people then came and planted. A real achievement."*

She vividly recalled the hard work that went into transforming the muddy fields into the attractive wildlife habitat of today. *"Another real success was the first time we were able to walk all the way round the meadows. At first you were stopped by huge, thick clumps of nettles and brambles in Meadow Three, so you could not appreciate the view*

Chapter Nine

looking back along the river. Now it's my favourite view; with your back to the river there are no buildings in sight."

By 2000 work in the Nature Reserve was really progressing. John Hyde had donated 120 trees, which were planted by Stan Stanistreet and form what is now called JohnStan Copse, to acknowledge the contribution they both made to the Reserve's development. By 2012 these trees had become a very attractive area of the reserve and have been underplanted with bluebells, snowdrops and aconites.

From the beginning, it was important to try to keep the paths open as vegetation grew very quickly. Trev Radford recalled, *"Ian Fisher was one of the early volunteers who worked hard on keeping the grass mowed."* A formal Management Plan was developed in 2001 by Mike Thomas, with help from the Ivel Valley Conservation Volunteers (IVCV) under Joel Carré and Cliff Andrews from Bedfordshire Rural Communities Charity (BRCC). Over the years, mainly due to the hard work of Teasel volunteers, the three fields of rough, muddy pasture have become a varied wildlife habitat, with native hedges of hornbeam and hawthorn, as well as copses of British trees, including oak, ash, beech, hazel, wild cherry and rowan. An osier bed was set up in Meadow Three and the stems are used by Sandra Barker – an internationally-famous, master basket maker, who lives locally – as well as for basketry workshops held at the Mill. The group receives additional help from Mick Dilley, who farms adjacent land and who trims the hedges and clears ditches.

The volunteers, often faced with little money to aid them, have shown great ingenuity. Louden Masterton recalled, *"When we were planting the hedge at the side of Meadow Two, we needed to make sure it was*

(Left) Geraldine Masterton and Frances Huckle putting in fencing. (Right) Louden Masterton and Keith Reynolds dragging logs from the river

well watered. Frances Huckle and I would manoeuvre a ten gallon barrel down to the river, dunk it in, seal the top and then roll it uphill to water the saplings."

Start-up money through P3 finally enabled the group to buy basic tools – bow-saws, billhooks, mattocks and spades – and to set up insurance. Additional finance came from IVCV and Rural Action Grants via BRCC. In later years there was funding from Stotfold Carnival and, after Paul Redwood became involved, from Stotfold Town Council, the Mill Preservation Trust and in 2008, £33,001.58 from Section 106 funding (from a new housing development nearby), all of which has enabled the group to buy more sophisticated tools and equipment and, more importantly, deliver the Nature Reserve and open it to the public.

There was at first a core of ten volunteers who worked every alternate Saturday morning from October to May and though the numbers have varied over the years, in 2012 there was an active group of fifteen who turn up regularly for work parties. Led by Patrick Chalmers and Valerie Balderstone, these volunteers, aided by members of the IVCV, have dug additional ponds of differing depths to encourage insect life, frogs, toads, newts and water birds.

One boundary of the meadows is formed by the River Ivel, which is being managed to maximise the habitat for endangered species like otters and water voles. Following reports that otters had been seen in the area, the volunteers put out special plasticine pads near the river and managed to capture paw prints, proving the animals do visit. In 2008 Louden Masterton found more evidence of these rare mammals. He reported, *"One morning in Meadow Three I came across a large pike lying on the path with its throat eaten in a semi-circle. I checked with BRCC, who confirmed it was definitely an otter and not a mink."* To encourage and safeguard otters visiting the Reserve, Teasel volunteers built an otter holt, one of two in Stotfold, along the Ivel.

A wildflower meadow was planted in the Autumn of 2010 and living willow bird hides have been set in place. Boardwalks enabling easy access to the wetter parts of Meadow Three were installed by the Ivel and Ouse Conservation

A view of the wildflower meadow in its first year

Chapter Nine

Volunteers under the direction of Cliff Andrews, who has provided significant conservation support and advice over the years. A car park with disabled spaces and a cycle rack were installed in 2009 and 2010 respectively.

Stotfold Mill Local Nature Reserve is now a vital part of the Bedfordshire and Luton Green Infrastructure Plan, creating a wildlife corridor along the course of the River Ivel. Corridors like this are becoming even more important as factors such as climate change and increased development force plants and animals to migrate. But, they are also good for people. Stotfold Town Plan, published in 2009, revealed that the majority of the population value their surrounding countryside and green places as a source of recreation and relaxation and felt it was extremely valuable to enhance their quality of life in the increasingly-crowded South East of the United Kingdom. The Nature Reserve has become an integral part of walking and recreation for the local area

BRCC volunteers starting to install the new boardwalk

Visitors surveying the largest pond from the completed dipping platform and residents and visitors from further afield comment on the delight they feel in having a wild space like this available to them.

Encouraging young people to enjoy their natural surroundings is an important aspect of Teasel's work and the ethos of the Nature Reserve. Pam Manfield and Stotfold Town Councillor Larry Stoter of the Nature Reserve Management Team contacted the local Bedfordshire, Cambridgeshire and Northamptonshire Wildlife Trust to ask for their help in setting up a Watch Group. Watch is the junior branch of the Wildlife Trusts and the UK's leading environmental action club for children. There are 300 groups around the country, aimed at young people aged 8-12, which provide, as the Watch website states, *'an exciting way to explore your surroundings and get closer to the wildlife you share it with'*.

After advertisements about the intention to set up a Watch group appeared in the town newsletter, the several potential leaders who came forward were taken to visit the award-winning Watch group at nearby Paxton Pits. Having seen the imaginative work done by that group and the obvious enjoyment of the children (and their accompanying parents) Gemma Waghorn agreed to become the first leader of the Stotfold Watermill Watch Group. Gemma was ideally suited for this role because of her background in Biology and work with local Scout groups.

The Wildlife Watch Group examining pond-dipping finds

Chapter Nine

She was joined as co-leader by Sue Clarke. As Sue confessed, both she and Gemma are *"keen on wildlife and the environment and know the importance of passing this on to our youngsters."* The group started in February 2011 with four children; by December they had 25 and a waiting list. A questionnaire in December 2011 discovered that most of the children (and their parents) enjoyed *'everything'*. There is a widely varying list of events as the 2012 programme demonstrated, from examining owl pellets to pond dipping, from making Christmas crafts out of wild materials, to guided tours of the Royal Society for the Protection of Birds Reserve in Sandy, as well as working on their own conservation area in the Nature Reserve.

The quality of the work involved in the Nature Reserve was first recognised in 2009 when the Campaign to Protect Rural England, Bedfordshire honoured Stotfold Watermill with its highest Living Countryside Award (the CPRE Mark) for landscape improvement in the Mill Meadows. In 2010 the team successfully applied for Local Nature Reserve status and later that year a Nature Reserve Management Team was set up under the chairmanship of Paul Redwood. The Reserve opened to the public on 2nd April 2011 and was formally declared open by Baroness Young of Old Scone on Sunday, June 5th of that year. A new Management Plan, Activity Plan, and various Policy Documents have all been created, to regulate the way in which the Reserve will be managed and developed.

The start of the Watch Group's conservation area in the Nature Reserve

The prestigious status of County Wildlife Site (CWS) was gained for Meadow Three in the Nature Reserve in October 2011, due to the importance of the habitat for water voles. (In fact all three species of mainland UK voles have been identified in the reserve.) CWS gives formal recognition of the value of the area for wildlife and so is a significant achievement in the transformation of the area into a rich wildlife habitat. In June 2012, the Nature Reserve gained the Green Flag Award – the national standard for parks and green spaces in the UK – which sets a benchmark of excellence in recreational green areas.

Mike Thomas commented, *"I feel proud of Meadow Three as it is now, and seeing the hedges and trees we planted growing to maturity. We did look at the long-term. Meadow Two was planned so we could have trees which would provide Autumn colour first and then the ones that would become long-lived standards, like the oaks. Often people don't see the long-term view but it is important to have this planning for planting. It's taken a while for Meadow Two to come through but it is now largely as we planned and it looks good."* He added, *"From the beginning though the work was secondary and Teasel was primarily a social group, which it still is, despite the large amount of work it has undertaken."*

In 2012 the Nature Reserve Management Team, still chaired by Paul Redwood, comprised Lyndsey Bignell, Countryside Officer for Central Bedfordshire Council; Patrick Chalmers, representing Teasel; Ray Kilby, a Mill Trustee; Richard Lawrence, Ecologist with Bedfordshire Rural Communities Charity; Pamela Manfield, Volunteer Co-ordinator for the Mill and Secretary of Teasel; and Councillor Larry Stoter, the Stotfold Town Council representative.

Local schoolchildren and volunteers from Acorn joined in the first Haymaking Day

Chapter Nine

At the time of writing, Teasel is working on achieving County Wildlife Site status for Meadow Two by increasing the biodiversity, particularly increasing the number and variety of wild flowers present and creating small haystacks to encourage grass snakes to breed on site, as well as providing shelter for hibernating insects and amphibians. The first Stotfold Haymaking Day was held in September 2012 when Teasel volunteers, joined by colleagues from Acorn, the conservation group in Arlesey and children from local schools, raked the cut hay and piled this into informal heaps. Teasel volunteers continue to donate time on a regular basis to ensure that the Nature Reserve is managed effectively for wildlife and for human visitors.

TEASEL STEERING GROUP 2012:

Valerie Balderstone; Patrick Chalmers; Pamela Manfield; Louden Masterton; Paul Redwood; Keith Reynolds

Team Members: Saul Ackroyd; Elizabeth Anderson; Nora Beale; Martin Bird; Geoff Bounds; Heather Chalmers; Zoe Channon; Pat Clarey; Lucy Clarke; Paul Clifton; Penny Daffarn; Jonathan Davidson; Ruth Featherstone; Richard Finch; Roger Finch; Dave Green; Darren Hammond; Jean Hill; Charles Howlett; Frances Huckle; Geraldine Masterton; Madeleine Mutton; Marianne Myhill; Gerry Newham; Lindsay Reynolds; Helen Vooght-Rogers; Roger Watson; Clare Whitty

Volunteers wearing the distinctive Teasel outfits sponsored by Satchells. Left to right: Geoff Bounds; Madeleine Mutton; Roger Finch; Valerie Balderstone; Louden Masterton; Frances Huckle; Richard Finch; Patrick Chalmers; Roger Watson; Heather Chalmers; Lindsay Reynolds; Helen Vooght-Rogers; Keith Reynolds

PART II: KEEPING THE WHEELS OF HISTORY TURNING

Raising funds for the rebuilding of the Mill and the creation of the Nature Reserve was a demanding and vital task, and required significant work for each grant application, and some ingenuity about where and how to apply. Today there is the equally demanding task of finding money for running costs. The Mill and Nature Reserve need about £23,000 each year to enable them to keep going and this would be impossible without the support of so many volunteers.

Pamela Manfield, who is Volunteer Co-ordinator for the Mill, said, *"As a guide to visitors, I thought I knew a fair amount about the effort involved in the restoration of the Mill and the creation of the Nature Reserve. The research for this book has really revealed to me the astounding courage and determination of the first volunteers, faced with a soot-blackened ruin and three muddy fields. Through my role as Volunteer Co-ordinator, I am also amazed at the number of people involved in the project and the skills, talents and hard work they bring.*

We do not have any paid staff. All the work is done by volunteers, who give up their time for a project about which they care deeply. It, therefore, seemed vital that the second part of this book would document the volunteer effort that goes into keeping the wheels of history turning."

Part of the management plan to try to ensure long-term sustainability, was the creation of teams of volunteers to specialise in particular areas of work. The amount of time given varies, depending on personal, family and work commitments. Some volunteers only help out at the two main fundraising weekends in the year, the Steam Fair and Country Show in May and the October Working Steam Weekend, while others specialise in helping provide support on the Sundays on which the Mill is open or for special group visits by schools, history societies etc. Many volunteers work in several teams and these are constantly expanding to new areas as need arises. In 2012 the major teams were:

Archive Team: record, preserve and display the documents and objects that form the Mill's history. Also devise special exhibitions to attract visitors.

Education Team: work with visiting schools to help children enjoy and appreciate the Mill and Nature Reserve.

Guides Team: provide friendly, knowledgeable information to visitors, at open Sundays and/or weekday group visits.

IT/website Team: ensure the technology is running effectively and publicise Mill events to the outside world.

Kingfisher Shop Team: source quality local art, crafts and produce and sell these to raise funds. Also sell the Mill's quality stone-ground flour, oats and bran and find additional outlets for these.

Maintenance Team: maintain the building and equipment and ensure the Mill is safe, tidy and welcoming.

Major Events Team: the wide range of volunteers who help to make the May Steam Fair and October Working Steam Weekend so successful and the smaller steering group which provides overall organisation.

Marketing Team: produce imaginative posters, leaflets, press releases, publicity (including Facebook) and put on a wide variety of events which attract visitors from increasingly further afield.

Milling Team: ensure the machinery runs efficiently and that the Mill's quality stone-ground flour and other products are produced regularly.

Millers Wheel Team: recruit new volunteers, run social events and organise the volunteer database.

Randalls Tea Room Team: provide a friendly, efficient catering service - preparing and sourcing delicious food, serving customers and, of course, washing up.

Small Events Team: develop a varied programme of events from workshops to concerts, to bring in visitors. Also publicise the Mill at outside events and run craft events for children.

Teasel: carry out conservation work on the Nature Reserve, as well as the other green areas of Stotfold.

Stotfold Art Group also works closely with both the Mill and Teasel.

This book was intended to depict the Mill and Nature Reserve twenty years after the great fire. Teams and activities are constantly changing, but the following chapters cover what was happening in 2012.

(Editors' Note: *No apostrophe is used in either Millers Wheel or Randalls Tea Room. This was a marketing decision for clarity of posters etc.*)

CHAPTER TEN

THE ARCHIVE TEAM

The Archive Team was set up in September 2009 with the aims of creating a core group of volunteers to work on the artefacts and papers related to the Mill; setting priorities; contacting specialists for advice or assistance; establishing a conservation and display policy for items based in the Mill and eventually applying for accreditation as a museum. Carolyn Monaghan admitted, *"I attended a training course – a SHARE Documentation Meeting – from which I came back thinking I can't do this. It's impossible; too complicated."* However, she bravely decided to go ahead and following a volunteer evening at the Mill, recruited Keith Reynolds, Roger Watson and Geoff Hoile as additions to the team. In 2011 they were joined by Richard Whitelock, whose model-making skills have been a great asset.

Roger Watson and Richard Whitelock of the Archive Team, together with Jean Kersey of Millers Wheel, admire a finished display of millworking tools

Chapter Ten

Work began with taking an inventory to include all artefacts which had been donated or were already in the Mill, except the fixed working machinery. Keith and Geoff also took photos of everything. Each object was numbered and Geoff entered the data on a computer.

Help was available via a booklet from SHARE, Support Help and Advice from Renaissance England, an organisation which shares time, expertise and resources across two hundred museums in the East of England, with the aim of protecting collections, improving services to visitors and building strong sector co-operation. Additional practical support and advice came from very useful visits from Libby Finney, previously Conservation Officer at St Albans Museum (in 2012 Conservator, Museum of London) and from Jenny Oxley, Curator of Mill Green, part of Welwyn/Hatfield Museum Group. Both of them, as Carolyn gratefully noted, *"helped with documentation, visited to sort out problems and were always at the end of an email to give advice."*

It took until the end of 2009 to ensure everything was cleaned. Because the team was dealing with historic items, it was important that proper materials were used. These include a range of specialist cleaning items, bought from a firm in North London – expensive but vital. Carolyn explained, *"One cleaner is great for rust removal, there is a lovely metal cleaner and Renaissance wax is used for coating unvarnished wood and stopping dust. These are used by the National Trust and Buckingham Palace, so we're in good company. My favourite item is the general cleaner used to get dirt off mucky old things that look as though they have been left in farmyards for generations."*

With cleaning complete, the formal process of accessioning items to the Mill's museum could start, with all items being individually marked – despite the difficult conditions. Carolyn commented, *"It was so cold sometimes we had to put a heater on to dry the marking fluid. It is a very fiddly and detailed job, with lots of sequential, time-consuming work; you need to be so methodical. Cleaning, marking and labelling takes a huge amount of time and it must seem to outsiders that we haven't done anything. Huge credit is due to Keith Reynolds and Roger Watson who have been absolutely brilliant at cleaning, marking and recording all our material. The documentation and computer recording of items have been vital steps towards museum accreditation".*

In 2010 when it was obvious that items would need to be shown to the public, Doug Pearson managed to acquire two free display cabinets from the British Schools in Hitchin. Carolyn said, *"The cabinets were ideal for our purpose, though they first needed a good clean. We didn't have a lot to display, so we put in what we had, ready for the start of the Mill opening for the new season".*

Carolyn Monaghan and Roger Watson at work cataloguing items

To gain ideas for displaying historic items, Carolyn went to a SHARE Display Course at Stockwood Discovery Centre in Luton which was *"brilliant. I got lots of ideas about how to write text and got a lovely little kit to make boards for text. It really explained how to set things up; they were a really good design team and very helpful".*

Keith Reynolds computerising the records

At the end of 2010 the team were starting to see results, the artefact descriptions were up and the display cabinets filled. Then some other bigger cabinets became available from Wardown Park Museum in Luton. The group was told that if they could collect the cabinets, they could have them for free, so *"John Saunders rounded up some helpers and organised delivery"*. The cabinets were very big and very heavy but it was thought they would just be able to fit through the Mill doors. However, the collection team returned *"with a few crushed toes and a cut hand"*, to find the

Chapter Ten

cabinets were actually too big to get into the Mill, so they spent a cold winter sitting in a truck. In January 2011 Ray Kilby decided to have another attempt. He took some doors off, made a pulley, removed some mouldings and, after considerable effort, finally managed to get the cabinets in. Carolyn said *"It was so dreadful and I felt so bad because they were really heavy. However, we got them in, and they're not moving now."*

The cabinets were cleaned and Carolyn bought some bargain cotton from John Lewis to line them. As she had never set up display cabinets before, she used her artistic and retail background and *"hoped for the best"*. There was not much time to prepare a display before the Mill opening season, so only the smock exhibit was ready. The Spur Wheel display took a lot of work, until that was finally put on show in late 2011.

In addition to the artefacts, the Mill has also acquired a huge document archive, including many of the Randall's papers, donated by Geraldine Dawson, who had attempted to put them in chronological order. There are also lots of photographs, plus maps and boxes of items from George Randall's house. Documents are currently mostly related to the Randalls, but *"other bits and pieces turn up"*. In the same way as the artefacts, each item is numbered, described, measured, categorised, has its condition assessed, and has its content listed as to what light it throws on the history of the Mill or the area. This is slow and cumulative work, though as papers are mostly solicitors' letters, often referring to bills a more complex story can be built up.

The Archive Team deal with both a museum process and a history process for paper objects. There is, first of all, a rough reading and interpretation of each item before it is entered into an accession book, a record card and a computer record. Then the object is put into special polypockets and finally into a Museum-grade storage box. Carolyn explained, *"We are lucky if we can do ten in a morning, plus heated discussions, on a good day."* A lot of 18th and 19th century items deal with the manorial system where copyhold was held by the Lord of the Manor and a lot of archaic terms are used, though *"They do become more familiar. Some papers are personal and these are more straightforward."* It had been difficult to work out how to display the many documents in the archive until Roger Watson suggested dividing them into two topics: the Mill and the community and the Mill in the outside world. These two strands made sense of the documents by putting them in context.

Carolyn stated, *"There is a lot of background work, but not what people notice. We have to change the displays and make the most of what we have got. It's a lot of work but it is interesting and I've enjoyed it. Keith and*

Roger have really got stuck in and had brilliant ideas and Richard has become a great additional asset. There is a lot of banter while we work!"

In 2011, Terry Brain, a solicitor from Biggleswade who was visiting the Working Steam Weekend, mentioned that as his firm were solicitors to the Randall family, he had an old box full of documents relating to the Mill, which he then donated to the Mill Trust. The earliest paper is dated 1734 and these documents, many on parchment, have done much to fill in the background history of the ownership and varying fortunes of the Mill through the 18th and 19th centuries, including details of fires, bankruptcies and family disputes. They were assessed and recorded by Pamela Birch of Bedfordshire and Luton Record Service. Pamela, born and brought up in Stotfold, has given a significant amount of time and expertise to help in this vital area.

Also in 2011 two new major exhibits joined the permanent displays at the Mill. The first was a unique piece of craftsmanship, by Carol Werrett – an exquisite, meticulously-researched, hand-crafted recreation of a 19th century miller's smock.

The Mill had been looking for a special exhibit to show visitors how different milling life would have been in past ages. Paul Redwood, then

A close-up of the completed smock, showing the fine detail of the work

Chapter Ten

a Trustee of the Mill, said, *"We wanted something to excite visitors' imaginations and knew it would have to be perfectly recreated. I had seen many examples of Carol's wonderful embroidery and dress-making and hoped she would agree to design and make a smock, but wondered if she would be prepared to take on this huge task."*

Carol did not hesitate to become involved and months of painstaking research followed, as she searched the Internet, visited museums, talked to curators and tracked down specialist companies to find authentic material and threads. She started her re-creation in November 2007 and continued despite increasing ill-health, which caused muscle loss in her hands. Her husband Bob recalled, *"The coarse material was hard to push a needle through, but Carole was determined to carry on. She found the best way was to do a little bit, rest and then pick it up again. Everything she did, she gave one hundred percent to it."*

The smock, now proudly displayed in its own cabinet, has detailed panels of traditional ears of wheat and other items associated with milling and is faithfully reproduced, even down to hand-turned wooden buttons (fittingly made by Ray Kilby, part of the current milling team at Stotfold Watermill). The material is a special hemp weave, which absorbs flour dust and would have provided the miller with extra warmth. The exquisite embroidery includes smocking on the front and even feather stitching round the hem.

Sadly Carol was unable to finish the smock before her death on December 31st 2009. Her daughter, Julie Speltinckx, who inherited her mother's creativity in needlework, decided she would like to finish the smock in memory of her mother, so the finished result is very much a joint effort.

Bob and his daughter have also donated Carol's working file – including detailed sketches, measurements and her correspondence in search of authentic items – to the Stotfold Mill Archive. Carolyn Monaghan said, *"The smock is a wonderful addition to the historical displays at the Mill and one which visitors are amazed by. The delicacy of the embroidery and the attention to detail make it a really special exhibit."*

The second major acquisition in 2011 is another tribute to the skills of local people – a minutely-detailed, scale-model of the mill, all of which is in working order. Created over a period of two years by Ray Kilby, the four foot high model is complete down to the weather-vane on the roof and the representation of the miller dressed in his characteristic waistcoat and bowler hat.

The model is not only a triumph of scale and detail, but of creative recycling. The space between the floors is composed of metal tubes

The Archive Team

Ray Kilby's intricate model of the Mill

Chapter Ten

from an old greenhouse and overflow pipes. Ray had to look for a long time to find something suitable for making the tiny, complex gears, ending up with three from wheel-brace hand-drills, while the biggest gear for the Spur Wheel came from a child's toy. Recreating the sack hoist that lifts sacks through the three floors of the Mill was also a problem, since as Ray explained, *"Little belts don't work like big belts. Small belts tend to be circular and the sack hoist belts need to be pear-shaped so they do not interfere with the work of the pulleys which run them. Eventually, a chain from a Lego toy provided the answer."*

For the scale model of the Mill, Ray had to work out the varying speeds of the gears and then by trial, error and creative recycling made things work. The engine which operates most of the machinery is an electric motor from an old toy and until the final test, Ray was not sure that this would be strong enough to work the model's complex machinery. His meticulous concentration on getting details right is shown in the sack hoist – which pulls the miniature sacks of flour up at exactly the right speed – and the fact that the water wheel moves exactly in proportion to the full-size Mill wheel. The model does have a few differences from the real Mill. Spaces between the floors have been enlarged to ensure that visitors can appreciate all the working parts and not just see the outside. Also, the concentration is on the working elements, so visitor attractions like the Tea Room and Gift Shop have been omitted.

Ray has also made two bespoke cabinets to fit in the lobby areas on the Stone and Dressing Floors, which provide much-needed additional display space. The colourful panels on these, showing the Milling and Maintenance Team at work, have been painted by Geoff Hoile.

Besides ensuring the documents and artefacts relating to the Mill are preserved for future generations, the work of the Archive group also enables special exhibitions to be mounted throughout the year, adding interest for visitors and enhancing their enjoyment of the Mill and the rural context in which it operated. In 2012 these included a Fire and Dereliction display based on material collected for this book; Stotfold at War and a Randall Family History Exhibition. New exhibits appear for each open season, and the displays in the Mill are constantly updated and amended by the team.

ARCHIVE TEAM 2012:

Leader: Carolyn Monaghan

Team Members: Roger Watson; Keith Reynolds; Richard Whitelock

CHAPTER ELEVEN

THE EDUCATION PROGRAMME AND GUIDES TEAM

Once the work on the Mill building was reaching completion, it was obvious that there was a need to help visitors, particularly children, make the most of their time in the Mill. Clare Whitty said, *"I was a Teasel member at first and had seen the Mill develop but only had time to get involved when I finished working. I had taught infant and junior children at various local schools, including St Thomas More in Letchworth, plus two terms in St Mary's in Stotfold and before I retired was Head of the Preparatory Department at St Francis College in Letchworth. Out of the blue I got a phone call from Paul Martin, asking if I had, or could get, a copy of the current Health and Safety booklet for schools visiting the Mill. I went to a meeting at Robin Tasker's house and various teams sat round the dining table: Tea Room, Marketing and so on, with Lorelie taking notes. I thought I was just there to bring my Health and Safety booklet, but suddenly I was the Education person. It was a bit of a shock, but I haven't regretted it for a moment."*

Clare was quickly joined by Patricia How, who had a love of local history and was very enthusiastic. They worked together for several months, until Patricia realised that the Mill would be open on Sunday, which would clash with her family and Church commitments, so reluctantly she dropped out. However, Pat Clarey, who had recently retired as chemistry teacher and Deputy Headmaster of the Priory School, Hitchin saw an advert for guides, joined the team and, as Clare put it *"We've been a great team since then."*

Pat and Clare first worked on ideas for school visits and produced worksheets, which Paul Redwood formulated into an Education Pack. Clare commented, *"We visited other museums to glean ideas and put together a plan to show off our Mill. We applied for anything with funding or that donated specialist time or goods to help. We were always the keen volunteers, prepared to try out new ideas."*

Chapter Eleven

They sent information out to all schools in a wide area of North Hertfordshire and Southern Bedfordshire, and then held discussion sessions with staff from local schools, from which significant links have developed. Clare stated, *"Pat and I get on really well and have the same ideas, which all helps. I used to teach children up to the age of eleven and Pat did the big boys and girls, but Pat has now become an expert in 'The Little Red Hen' story that we use with the infants – and I'm in my element. It's important for the children to have a male member of staff around and it's good when the millers join in as well, as they are absolutely wonderful, especially Phil Radford and Ray Kilby. They really get involved with the little ones, which form the majority of our school visits."*

Because of health and safety arrangements and the cost of transport, it is often difficult for schools to organise outside visits, but Stotfold schools have been very supportive, especially Roecroft School, through the connection with Ray Kilby, and St Mary's, where Clare used to teach. There have also been visits from St Thomas More Roman Catholic Primary School and St Francis College, Letchworth and, since one of the teachers at St Francis also works at St Christopher's, they now come on visits also. As Clare put it, *"We have to use our contacts wherever possible. We include the Nature Reserve as well as the Mill on visits. Most schools who have visited know what the Mill has to offer, but for new schools we invite a teacher to visit first, take them on a tour and then ask what area of the curriculum they want to work on. We try to tailor our input based on that conversation."*

Both Pat and Clare commented that one of the most enjoyable parts of the Education Programme has been the development work with Lonsdale School, a special school for children with physical and mental impairments. Following a very successful visit by Claudia Thiele, a teacher at Lonsdale, the school has worked closely with the Mill and a number of excellent visits have followed. Pat recalled one very severely handicapped student, who was blind, deaf, in a wheelchair, permanently on a drip and who only communicated

Pat Clarey explaining how grain is fed into the millstones

The Education Programme And Guides Team

Clare Whitty telling stories to a group of school children

with her carer through touch. *"I wondered, what this child would get out of a visit but she had a great day. The highlight was when bread dough was put in her hands, so she could feel the texture and she loved it."* He added, *" An experience like that really makes you feel that what you're doing is worthwhile."*

Clare commented, *"Children generally love the hand quern where they can grind their own flour and they find the waterwheel fascinating. They go away with the idea that the place is fun and exciting – there's noise and movement and the millers really involve them. We have children from Lonsdale School in wheelchairs and with other disabilities and Phil Radford has a special rapport with them. People can always tell if someone really enjoys working with children. The Tea Room ladies are very sociable and it all adds to the atmosphere."*

The children have obviously been stimulated by their visits and Lonsdale school has produced lots of material about the Mill, notably 'Who wants to be a Stotfold Millionaire?' and 'How a Mill works'.

Pat Clarey's wife, Anne, a former Home Economics teacher, was drawn into the Education Programme to provide demonstrations of bread making. She makes various doughs, displays different types of flour

Chapter Eleven

and talks about gluten and where flour comes from. Once the dough is mixed, the children and carers are encouraged to handle it. Anne added, *"All the way through the programme, in the background, a loaf of bread is cooking – on the longest session the maker allows. Then there is a silent two minutes, while everyone waits for the ping when the bread is done. I give a safety talk about taking the bread out and then they take the loaf back to school with jam from the Tea Room and have jam sandwiches for tea."*

Links with the local museum services proved very important for development of the education programmes. Funding from the Bedfordshire Museum Services provided a large amount of resources for use with schools, including very colourful play mats and the loan boxes that schools may borrow. These contain pictures, samples, worksheets and even a modern quern that teachers can use in class to teach about mills and flour production.

The Mill is part of the Museums Education Forum, which has provided both funding and resources. The Museums Service were worried that visitor numbers were falling and that museums were not relevant, so community outreach had been suggested. Fatima Choudhury a former history teacher from Luton was given the task of initiating the programme and as Clare said, *"This made a big change and was a real catalyst to get us going. The help was mutually beneficial as Fatima was keen to help us while the Mill was eager for*

Anne Clarey showing pupils from Lonsdale School how bread is made

input and potential funding. Meeting Fatima was the best thing that could have happened; she gets seven stars." Fatima, along with Jane Munns from the Hertfordshire Museum Service, became the key to the Museums Group, which included lots of other local organisations who were looking at attracting visitors, especially children and getting communities involved. Clare stated, *"I was delighted how group members were willing to share expertise and enthusiasm about their own museums. We were all volunteers – and a great range of ages – helping and sharing expertise and not vying for customers. We were all doing this for the love of it."* Pat recalled, *"We had a lot of support and encouragement from Fatima and Jane, who obtained the funding which enabled us to make the Milly Mouse Trail."*

Stotfold Watermill, Mill Green at Hatfield and Papertrail (a papermill at Hemel Hempstead) formed the Green Mill Group, which joined together to enhance their work with schools. The group developed the idea of producing a trail which children and parents could follow around each building, to promote the idea of museums as learning spaces and which would encourage parents to work with their children while visiting. For Stotfold Watermill, Pat came up with the concept of Milly the Mouse and a former colleague, Cherry Blackbourne, an art teacher, created the figure of Milly. The signs and leaflets featuring the little mouse have proved very popular with parents and children visiting the Mill at weekends.

Two further members of the team have been Reg Lyon and, more recently, Marlene Machell. As Pat said, *"Both have a great rapport with the groups of children visiting the Mill and are only too willing to give up their time to work with youngsters."*

The Education Programme continues to expand its remit. The Nature Reserve is proving an additional enhancement to many school visits and St Francis College has incorporated it into their curriculum for Year 4. Pat commented, *"We are hoping to find a volunteer with appropriate knowledge and skills to help take this development forward into the future."*

EDUCATION TEAM 2012:

Leaders: Pat Clarey; Clare Whitty

Team Members: Reg Lyon; Marlene Machell; Jan Ray and Joy Burton who has provided musical support on occasions.

Chapter Eleven

MILL GUIDES

From the very beginning of the restoration it was felt important both to involve and inform the local community and raise funds by encouraging visitors from further afield. At the beginning of their involvement, Pat and Clare also acted as guides for tour groups and Pat researched information on mills and the history of milling, producing pages of notes which are still used as the basis of guide training. Pat stated, *"I'm a chemist not a historian, but my research made me even more aware of the important links between mills, legislation and historical events – the 19th century Corn Laws, the Napoleonic Wars and social history generally."*

Clare said, *"Originally we held a slide show and then talked and took people on a tour with a small charge. Because we were only getting small numbers on the tours this stopped being practical, especially when there were a lot of other people in the mill, so we decided it would be better to have a guide on each floor who could talk about that area and answer questions and this seems to work well. The booked tours still get a slide show and are divided into groups with their own guide, but that is not a problem as they are the only visitors around. The coach tours are also enthusiastic about the Mill, the Tea Room and the Nature Reserve. We troop around the reserve in rain or whatever."*

Marlene Machell explaining displays on the Stone Floor to a school group

Reg Lyon providing information on the Stone Floor

The original two guides were soon joined by others, many of whom were already associated with the Mill in different roles and as Pat had produced the information sheets, he became *de facto* responsible for the Guides Team and has led it since then. He confessed, *"I was fascinated by the Mill and what people had achieved and felt an obligation to support it."*

Robert Smith, who is also responsible for many of the classic photographs of the Mill, each year revamps the slide presentation given to groups. He commented, *"Now we also have one in French, thanks to Tony Machell and one of my old teachers, specially produced for a visiting group from France in 2012."*

Alan Greenshields used to volunteer at the East Anglian Transport Museum when he lived on the East coast. In 2009 he brought friends from Lincoln to the October Steam Weekend and filled in a volunteer form, as he had been an engineer and thought his skills might help. He commented, *"I've been coming ever since and help out wherever I can, but mostly with guiding. Now I'm retired I have the time. They're a smashing group of people and I've really been welcomed. I love watching the machinery running as I worked with gears all my life.*

Chapter Eleven

Jean Kersey who also joined the team in 2011 said, *"What I enjoy most is meeting so many interesting people from all different walks of life, while helping to preserve such a wonderful piece of our heritage. I love being a guide as I learn something new every time."*

Brian Saunders worked in the Car Parking Team on Major Events weekends for many years, before he joined the Guides Team in 2011. He said, *"I'm not technical, so I particularly enjoy the Meeter and Greeter role, where you really find out what people have enjoyed about their visit. The Mill has enthusiastic volunteers who work there because they love what they're doing and that comes across to visitors."*

Clare Whitty said, *"What do I get out of it? The sheer enjoyment of going to the Mill and being part of the community, learning something new and stimulating and using skills I might have left behind when I retired. I've seen it grow over the years and I really enjoy the people who come to visit. For me, it's important that it's brought together people who have different skills and are willing to share them. We work as a team and even if we don't want to do something, we will do it, if we feel it's needed. We're all here to help, to encourage others to share our enthusiasm for a Mill which has been brought back to life by volunteers. It has become the focus of a lot of people to volunteer their time and for the wider community to enjoy. That's why the free admission is important – it belongs to everyone."*

Pat Clarey concluded he particularly enjoyed two things about his connection with the Mill, *"learning more about the historical background and especially working with people, both in the Mill in various teams and with visitors – passing on the things I have found fascinating."*

His Guides Team obviously succeed in communicating their love of the Mill. A recent visitor from Canada stopped to thank the guide nearest the front door, *"because all of you have so much passion for this place and its history."*

GUIDES TEAM 2012:

Leader: Pat Clarey

Team Members: Pat Coffey; Ed Clutten; Alan Greenshields; Jean Kersey; Reg Lyon; Marlene Machell; Pam Manfield; Louden Masterton; Helen Moore; Doug Pearson; Jan Radford; Jan Ray; Brian Saunders; Robert Smith; Clare Whitty; Hilary Woods

CHAPTER TWELVE

FRIENDS OF THE MILL AND MILLERS WHEEL

To help in raising funds and to keep the volunteers motivated, the 2002 Annual General Meeting proposed the setting up of *Friends of the Mill*, with an annual subscription of £5, a newsletter every two months and free entry to the Mill. Members were invited to be involved in the 'democratisation' of the Trust, to use their skills and to help with work in the Mill.

Mary Pateman had moved to the house next door to John Hyde in 2000 and *"was aware of John's great enthusiasm for everything to do with the Mill"*. After she was made redundant in 2001 and *"had loads of time"* she was soon recruited to help extend the volunteer programme, though she admitted her first meeting with Christine Smith and John Hyde was, *"so scary as there was so much to be done. Christine made suggestions on how she would like the volunteer programme*

The Millers Wheel tent at the Steam Fair, manned by volunteers

Chapter Twelve

to run and gave me a list of people to tell about our plans and to ask for support, whether physical help at events or to raise money. At the first Steam Fair I can remember standing in the field thinking how amazing this was."

A major part of the work of Friends of the Mill (now Millers Wheel) is recruiting enough volunteers to ensure the effective running of the two major fund-raising events, the May Steam Fair and Country Show and the Working Steam Weekend, held in October of every year. As Mary said, *"We were constantly trying to get more people as we expanded. We put items in 'The Comet' and other local papers and did manage to get people. On open days we had a volunteer leaflet to encourage people to volunteer."* As well as, or instead of, active help, people could support the Mill financially by donating £10 per person per year to Mill funds and this practice still continues, even after the name change.

In later years, there has also been the need to provide a steady input of new volunteers for the increasing number of activities that occur at other times, especially the Sunday afternoons when the Mill is open to the public and the evening events put on by the Small Events Team.

Mary Pateman ran Friends of the Mill and worked on the Major Events Team *"until I left because it was such a big job and conflicted with family commitments. The organisation had got bigger, we needed more regular get-togethers and I'm not computer-minded. I did everything the old-fashioned way. Friends of the Mill took over my dining room and I'd spend every week working on it. I knew every member on first name terms. We had 70 volunteers in my time, but it was clear we needed a more professional person if we were going to expand enough."*

She added, *"I gained great friendships from all this. I used to keep a calendar of what we had been and what we had become. It's really impressive how a small community can do something so fantastic."*

Mary handed over the organisation to Jo and Andrew Towler who had moved into the newly-built Mill View, along the road from the Mill. They greatly expanded the recruitment of volunteers, especially via the Friends of the Mill stall at major weekend events, until family circumstances made this impossible. Mary commented, *"The Towlers did some wonderful work, including running a very successful cheese and wine evening."*

Following an advertisement in the town's newsletter, *Stotfold News*, asking for a new Volunteer Co-ordinator, Peter Hollingsworth was recruited in 2008 and remained in the post until 2010. As he had a wide experience as secretary of various local organisations, he was an extremely useful asset to the Mill. Peter introduced a supporters' database and refined the volunteer recruitment leaflets. He held Volunteers' Evenings to attract new people and at one of these recruited Roger Watson, who became Database Manager. Peter said, *"I really enjoyed the interaction with people and seeing them get involved with the Mill."* Finding that the post involved rather more time than had been anticipated, after two years, Peter relinquished the role.

As the number of volunteers grew, the collection of annual membership dues and the distribution of membership cards became too difficult, so the system changed to one where all regular volunteers or donors became automatic members of the newly-named Millers Wheel.

Pamela Manfield was recruited as Volunteer Co-ordinator at the beginning of June 2010, following her early retirement. She had first helped out with car parking at the May weekend, but was persuaded by Jo Towler to become involved in other aspects. After an interview by then Trustee Paul Redwood, she joined the Sustainable Development Team, and amongst other projects, led the team which produced the first Mill Guidebook in 2009, before taking over the Volunteer Co-ordinator role. She had had considerable experience in working with volunteers from previous employment both in the UK and the United States.

Pam Manfield and Pat Clarey in discussion with Deputy Lord Lieutenants at the QAVS Award Ceremony

Chapter Twelve

(Left) Jean Bean stocking up on Mill leaflets (centre) Simon Law in the Mill entrance at Christmas and (right) Lynn Roper still providing tea for volunteers

Together, she and Paul Redwood created the Volunteer Handbook which provides new volunteers with information about the Mill and its history, a volunteer induction programme and details the respective responsibilities of both the Mill and the new volunteers. She has spear-headed role descriptions for all volunteers, enabling the Mill to seek new helpers via the Community Service Volunteer offices in Bedford and North Hertfordshire. Volunteer recruitment leaflets have been created, showing the wide variety of roles on offer, since the Mill now has a number of teams of volunteers working in different areas.

Roger Watson has masterminded the management of the Millers Wheel database, which enables the team to keep up-to-date records of all volunteers and records all hours donated to the Mill over the year. It also enables most of the volunteers to be kept in touch with Mill events through emails, as well as the Millers Wheel newsletter. Roger's figures demonstrated that, in 2012, the 165 active Mill volunteers racked up an impressive 10,700 hours, which at the standard rate used by the government for calculating volunteer time was the equivalent of over £120,000. Since many volunteers are very highly skilled, this estimate could easily be doubled. Roger's work also makes it simpler to contact volunteers for individual teams needed for the two major fundraising weekends. Since 2011 he has taken over the huge task of organising the complex volunteer rotas needed to ensure that all aspects of activity are properly staffed.

Roger moved to nearby Arlesey in 2004 from Borehamwood and as he said *"I was winding down my job and thinking about early retirement. Peter Hollingsworth was looking for somebody to help set up the computer records on a more organised basis, so I offered*

Friends Of The Mill And Millers Wheel

to help. That was about the time when we changed from an annual subscription for membership, to the current system that all active volunteers are members of Millers Wheel. I finally retired in 2010 so, as I then had more time, became involved in the Archive Group and Teasel, as well as the Millers Wheel Team."

He added, *"I've been lucky to be able to contribute to the Mill in a number of different ways, using and developing a variety of skills, so volunteering makes me feel useful. I enjoy the challenges and working with a great bunch of people, especially seeing how the results of our work is appreciated by visitors and the local community."*

Jean Kersey, who joined in 2011 when she moved back to Stotfold, has taken over responsibility for managing the social programme for volunteers and organising the Mill presence at outside events. The Millers Wheel stall sells flour and publicises the activities of the Mill and forthcoming events, while children (and their parents) are encouraged to try using the hand quern to grind their own flour. It provides an ideal opportunity to widen the breadth of visitors and, hopefully, to acquire new volunteers. Jean commented, *"I filled in a volunteer form and got talking to Pam at the Millers Wheel stall at a May event and that was it. Joining Millers Wheel seemed like a good way to get to know people in the town; little did I realise how*

Teasel celebrating the opening of the Nature Reserve in 2011. Paul and Joyce Redwood opening the champagne, with Kevin Balderstone in the background

Chapter Twelve

involved I would become and how much fun it would be. I've always firmly believed that the more you put in to something the more you get out of it. That's certainly true of the Mill. Being a volunteer here has most definitely played a big part in helping me settle into my new life in Stotfold."

The team was completed by Lucy Clarke whose talents for publicity and computer skills were employed in creating imaginative posters for events, providing news and photographs for the managers of the Mill website and the Mill screens and ensuring the Facebook site gets lots of up-to-date news to circulate. Lucy and her husband, John, moved to Stotfold in 2006 and Lucy recalled, *"About four hours after we moved into our new home, our next door neighbours asked us round for drinks with some of their friends. Having over a hundred packing cases round us, of course we said 'yes'. That evening we met our neighbours' good friends Heather and Patrick Chalmers who were deeply involved with Teasel, as they still are. Heather did a great sales pitch and invited us to join them. This expanded into becoming a member of the Millers Wheel team and helping with other teams also."* She added, *"I get a great sense of achievement (and sometimes amazement) at how many varied volunteers keep the project moving forward."*

The Millers Wheel Team organises self-funding social events throughout the year for the current Mill volunteers and keeps them

Trustees and volunteers celebrating the Queen's Award, held by Christine Smith. L to R: Paul Redwood, John Saunders, Pam Manfield, John Hyde, Ron Roper, Jan Radford, Phil Radford, Trev Radford, Louden Masterton, Jackie Radford, Kevin Balderstone, Ray Kilby, Chris Foskett

informed of Mill activities through a quarterly newsletter. In addition, it actively recruits new volunteers through posters, stalls at the major Mill events and at outside events, like the Bedfordshire Steam Fair, as well as via local community groups. With the advent of email, relatively few volunteers and patrons now get information in paper form and those who do get their communications with the delivery assistance of Doug Pearson – and especially Chris Webster and her trusty bicycle.

Though the team's remit is only to cover their costs, they also manage to raise funds for the Mill and Nature Reserve, primarily through the annual Mill Quiz. Run by experts Lyn and Steve Hayes, the Quiz has become a firm favourite with many volunteers and teams from elsewhere. Lyn is renowned for the quirkiness of her questions, which have teams racking their brains over wide-ranging topics.

Formal recognition of the quality of the time and skills donated by volunteers to the restoration and sustainability of the Mill and Nature Reserve came in July 2010 with the Queen's Award for Voluntary Service, the MBE for voluntary organisations. The award – an engraved crystal obelisk – was fittingly presented to Ron Roper, representing the Mill volunteers, by Sir Samuel Whitbread KCVO, then Lord Lieutenant of Bedfordshire, on behalf of the Queen.

Hundreds of volunteers, past and present, came together to celebrate this extremely significant award gained by this volunteer-run charity. The ceremony was also attended by many prominent figures in local government, including three Deputy Lord-Lieutenants: Judith Howard, Anthony Ormerod and Brian Woodrow; Councillor Peter Hollick, Chairman of Central Bedfordshire; Councillor Tricia Turner, Leader of Central Bedfordshire Council; Councillor Brian Collier, Chair of Stotfold Town Council and the Town Clerk, Ms Kate Elliott-Turner. Also present was then County Councillor Christina Turner, who nominated the Mill for the award.

Alistair Burt, MP for North East Bedfordshire, who was sadly unable to attend, sent his congratulations and best wishes to the volunteers, adding, *"This is fitting recognition of an astounding achievement by a local community."*

MILLERS WHEEL TEAM 2012:

Leader: Pamela Manfield

Team Members: Lucy Clarke, Jean Kersey, and Roger Watson, with Pat Clarey and Christine Smith as Trustee members

CHAPTER THIRTEEN

INFORMATION TECHNOLOGY AND THE WEBSITE

Kevin Balderstone, the Trustee responsible for Health and Safety and the IT within the Mill, moved to Stotfold in 1979 when he got married. His first recollection of visiting the Mill after the fire was when *"there was still a tarpaulin over the water wheel."* He remembers his first volunteering role involved *"spending numerous hours perched on the wheel helping volunteers chip off the large deposits of lime scale which had formed on the wheel since the Mill had become derelict."*

In 2003 he answered the call for volunteers to help at one of the first May fundraising events. Kevin vividly remembered the 2004 May

Kevin Balderstone at work on the Mill computing system

Event. *"It really rained that year; I spent the whole weekend trying to contain the mud. Dave McIver and I spent two days collecting straw bales from a local farm in John Hyde's truck and scattering them in the event field in a vain attempt to try and soak up some of the water. In those days we used to have the Mill Ball on the Saturday night during the event and I still remember Dave and I, covered from head to toe in mud, on our knees, putting a green carpet down so people could get to the marquee without getting dirty. People were actually stepping over us as we were doing the finishing touches to the carpet. When we finished we had less than twenty minutes to get back home, shower and get changed into our dinner suits. I remember thinking, 'Do I really want to go back for the Ball?'"*

Kevin had been a school governor at Etonbury Middle School for 13 years, but when his children left secondary education, he decided to retire from this post. John Hyde seized the opportunity to get him involved with the Major Events Team and help with fundraising for the Mill. When the Steam Fair and Country Show was officially recognized by the National Traction Engine Trust, a Safety Officer was needed, so Kevin took on that role. He said modestly, *"It's a very grand-sounding title but basically I inherited the job because no-one else wanted to do it."* This involvement has continued.

In addition to his work with the Major Events Team, Kevin has also been deeply involved in introducing technology into the Mill. He took the opportunity, whilst the Mill was being rebuilt, to install a structured wiring system throughout the building. This cabling system has been used not only for the Mill computers but also for the CCTV and phone system which Kevin designed and installed. A single server was originally commissioned, running Windows SBS 2003 and provision was made for key volunteers to access the Mill server remotely from their own home computers. This server was later converted to a Terminal server and runs in conjunction with a new Windows-based server, which handles all the Mills computing needs and is still being used today.

Kevin said, *"Highlights of my time at the Mill have been seeing the water wheel run again for the first time since the fire. Also, being chairman of the Major Events Team and helping organise the 10th anniversary May Steam Fair and Country Show in 2012, which turned out to be the biggest and most profitable event Stotfold has ever seen. I did wonder if it would be the first event to lose money because of the constant bad weather in the preceding months."*

He added, *"I'm also very pleased with the technology I have introduced; without it I think we would struggle to run the Mill in the 21st century. Another memorable moment for me was being introduced to the Duke of Edinburgh at the official opening."* He continued, *"I like the fact that I'm putting something back into the community and helping to preserve part of Stotfold's heritage for future generations."*

Ed Clutten, Manager of the Mill's website (and also a member of the Guides Team) said, *"I got involved with the Mill when we moved to Stotfold in 2001. I had been working as a Computer Systems Designer, and when I heard about the Mill knocked at Robin Tasker's door and asked if he wanted a website set up."* At the time this was not a possibility as the Trust was applying for grants and there were worries that a fully-functioning website might adversely affect applications, by indicating that the project would go ahead with or without funding.

Ed continued, *"Two to three years later while playing golf, I met Kevin Balderstone, who mentioned that the Mill were looking for somebody to develop their website. There was a basic website in place, which Kevin had inherited and was trying to keep updated, but there was a desperate need for a new more comprehensive and intuitive site, and I was asked if I could take on the challenge and design a new website for the Mill. I had a formal interview with a lot of people and almost decided this was too much like being at work, but I did get involved and designed and installed a new website for the Mill. I have carried on since then."*

In 2011 Ed was joined by Lucy Clarke, whose role was to liaise with the various team leaders and volunteers to discover news items and updates for inclusion within the web site. The website, developed by Ed, has now become one of the key tools the Mill uses for publicising Stotfold Mill and attracting visitors.

CHAPTER FOURTEEN

THE KINGFISHER GIFT SHOP AND FLOUR SALES

The Kingfisher Shop opened in March of 2008, under the management of Carolyn Monaghan, with a focus on providing quality, preferably locally-sourced, art and craft work, as well as local produce, including that of the Mill itself. Carolyn was an ideal choice for Shop Manager as she had been employed by various large retail companies in the area, before she moved to part-time work for Oxfam in Letchworth. When this closed, she needed an outside interest, so after Paul Redwood asked her about taking on the Mill Shop *"it seemed an ideal opportunity"*. Carolyn drew up the plans for the shop, including the choice of paint colours and gave them to John Hyde to include in the building work.

When the Tea Room opened and before the shop was completed Jenny Musselwhite and Carolyn raised funds from *"a table in a draughty corridor"*. They sold mill merchandise and polo-shirts ordered via Christine Smith who knew about suppliers from working at Knebworth House and with advice from Lorelie Tasker. Craft suppliers were initially recruited from people who had stalls at the May fundraising weekends. Paul Redwood also helped as he had contacts from volunteering with the local Hospice where he ordered items for sale. They started with a small budget and a few items but were quite successful and by the end of 2007 the shop was finished and they could begin work in earnest.

Jenny recalled, *"Carolyn asked me to give her a hand to run sales of items. At first this was just a rail of T-shirts and a table with pens, pencils etc. When the shop was envisaged, I was asked to help with the planning, everything from scrubbing floors to finding stock. I do the craft side and contact local crafts people and collect stock from them. The decision on what we stock is made jointly and based on quality. As people drop out, new ones come in. We chose a country theme to fit the Mill and try to aim at variety and that stock is locally made – a radius of about ten miles."*

She added, *"I really enjoy meeting the different people we get as visitors, especially as they are always so interested in the Mill. We get such*

Chapter Fourteen

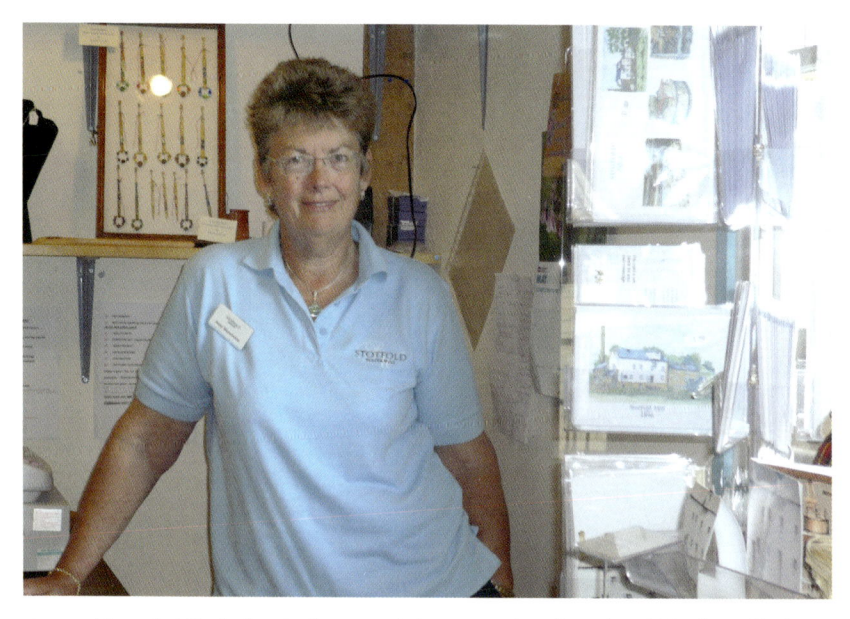

Jenny Musselwhite in front of some of the art and craftwork sold in the Gift Shop

nice comments from visitors too. Recently, there was a letter from a group who had visited, which especially thanked "the lovely lady in the Shop". Another of the group said, "It's just like the National Trust, only cheaper." I got involved because I believe old things have to be kept going, so future generations can see them. I think the Mill's future is secure as long as people keep coming in."

Carolyn admitted that her role was worrying at first. She had never ordered and customised items before or decided on core goods likely

Jan Radford's popular Mill Mice; some have travelled as far as Australia

126

to sell. *"It was a surprise. I hadn't expected to be doing this."* Christine Smith had some background experience and could give advice, but it was *"really a case of seeing what would sell – a big learning curve"*. There were only a few major flops, like the expensive chocolates ordered for the Christmas of 2008 – to coincide with the credit crunch when all major shops were making massive discounts. They were *"quite upmarket sweets and did not shift"*.

However, this was a rare occurrence and the Kingfisher Shop has become a significant fundraising source for the Mill. Carolyn commented, *"When I see people coming round the Mill and having a good day out, I really feel we are doing something enjoyable and worth while."*

Stotfold Watermill usually produces only two and a half tons of flour a year, as production is limited by storage space. Unlike traditional mills, the restored Stotfold Watermill has been adapted to cater for visitors, so safety barriers, a tea room, gift shop and a lift for visitors with disabilities have all limited the space available to keep large quantities of flour. In addition, since the Mill is not in frequent use during the winter months, keeping flour in good condition would be

Carolyn Monaghan talking with Reg Lyon in the well-stocked Gift Shop

Chapter Fourteen

Stotfold Watermill's distinctive flour bags

difficult and new health and safety regulations are strictly adhered to.

Since Carolyn used to work in major supermarkets she is well aware of the importance of food hygiene. Ray Kilby had recommended the Flour Advisory Board website, which explained how to set up a regulatory system with a certificate signed by the miller. Sacks are rotated in date order of milling with sequential month numbers. Each set of flour bags is numbered with the month on which it was produced, so it can be traced back. Also Carolyn has devised a sell-by date system, usually six months after the day of milling.

Carolyn explained, *"We sold flour from the start and first ordered bags and labels for the 2008 May Weekend. They were a real problem as they had to be stuck on by hand; the current ones are easier to separate and don't take as long. It was very labour intensive."* The major events pose particular problems, since large amounts of flour are needed. In 2011, 250 bags were supplied and sold over two days. Carolyn noted how important it is to keep pace with production of flour, so close collaboration with the milling team is vital.

Once the flour has been ground, it is put in sacks and moved to the Clean Room, in hoppers, so it is easier to manage. It is weighed out and put into bags, which are then sealed and numbered. Carolyn said, *"Tania Beale has done sterling work on flour bagging since joining the team in 2012. It is great to have someone you can rely on to do this important job well".* Flour sales have proved very popular and rolled oats and bran have been added to the range of products.

Kingfisher Gift Shop 2012

Leader: Carolyn Monaghan

Team members: Tania Beale, Jenny Musselwhite

CHAPTER FIFTEEN

LOCAL FUNDRAISING AND MAJOR EVENTS

From the start of the restoration, it was felt important not only to raise money, but also to inform and involve the local community. Until large amounts of grant funding were secured, the restoration work was dependent on local fundraising or the generosity of individuals. Small-scale fundraising was, in any case, vital to facilitate the larger grants, many of which required matching funds and was also needed to cover the costs involved in progressing grant applications.

In the early days the team were as much amateurs at raising money as they were at many of the other skills needed to save and restore

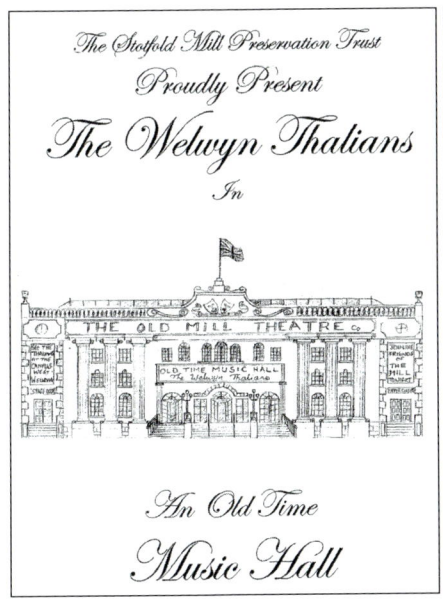

(Left) The programme of the Old Time Music Hall concert, designed by Trev Radford.
(Right) An early poster for what became the Steam Fair and Country Show

Chapter Fifteen

the Mill, so they were prepared to try all sorts of weird and wonderful ideas. Charcoal dug from the ruins of the Mill was bagged up and sold for use by local artists. Trev Radford remembered an auction, *"where Jan Chellew paid a fortune to buy back one of her husband Dave's jumpers and John Hyde did a partial strip."*

Trev organised a highly successful quiz evening at a local pub, complete with steak pie dinner and confessed, *"I loved doing the quiz despite the teasing I got from friends for always including a question on the TV show, Dad's Army."* Through his sister Jackie's membership, the Welwyn Thalians, a local amateur dramatics group, were persuaded to stage a series of Old Time Music Hall performances at the Memorial Hall. Trev recalled, *"These played to packed houses, boosted by the bar takings, though the unpredictability of choices meant that Adrian Morrow spent half the evening dashing out to local shops to avoid a lost sale when a member of the audience requested a drink that we didn't have in stock."*

They also ran Jumble Sales, the first of which was in fact a car boot sale at the Mill, with *"lots of odds and ends"*. For over thirty years, Chris Webster had run a Jumble Sale in Stotfold Carnival Week, and when this ended, asked Christine Smith if she would like the Sale to be run to raise funds for the Mill. The Jumble Sales have continued every year since and have raised thousands of pounds, as well as providing great local publicity. Chris said of her involvement, *"When walking in you always feel it's YOUR Mill, as everyone who works there feels a bit of pride; it's so special. Besides the Jumble Sale, I also work in the Tea Room, deliver newsletters and help at May and October events. I love doing it."*

The first Open Day was held on 13th and 14th of May 2000, to coincide with National Mills Weekend and Lynn Roper's work log recorded: *'Tidying up for the Mill's first open day! Descaling the waterwheel, clearing of stream, clearing away weeds and mowing grass at the front of the Mill.'* This event started in a very small way with a few stalls on trestle tables in what is now part of the Nature Reserve, selling plants, bric-a-brac, books, cakes and souvenirs and with a photographic exhibition about the Mill. Daisy File *"quite a*

Lorelie Tasker running a stall at an early fundraising event

character in the village" and Dorothy Lindsay were two stalwarts of the cake stall. There were also a few traction engines on show and Trev Radford ran a duck race, which was hugely popular with local children. Trev remembered that years later when he was walking round at a steam fair near Slough a complete stranger came up to him and said, *"You're the Duck Man"* – as Trev commented, *"an odd kind of fame!"*

Sheila Archer recalled, *"The first time I got involved we held one of the events in the field, no steam engines, just a trestle table with a homemade game, a long piece of paper, marked out in squares. If you threw a hoop on special squares, you won a gift. Lots of bric-a-brac too. I got involved because if I believe in something then I volunteer to help and I was cross because of the destruction from the fire. I've always been interested in history and this is a historic part of Stotfold. I always believed it would be a success. The important thing is what we're here for – the Mill. People will come and go but the Mill will be here forever."*

There was no proper roof on the Mill at the time, merely plastic sheeting nailed to temporary beams. Old table cloths were draped over the charred remnants that had once formed the floor of the Mill, creating a small booth which acted as a shop. Jan Radford and Chris Webster made tea for visitors on a camping stove balanced on a pile of bricks. To liven up (and disguise) the temporary corrugated iron roof, brightly coloured flags were flown from the front of the building, a custom followed at every May event since then. Trev recalled, *"We were so proud and excited that the Mill would be open for National Mills Weekend, even in its broken and battered state. It was still dangerous in parts. We couldn't let anyone go out the back as there were piles of bricks there. We weren't sure if anyone would turn up, so were surprised and delighted that so many people came and really did care about the Mill."*

Later that year, there was another fundraising event as John Hyde, the builder whose company rebuilt the Mill building, remembered. *"We set up a little fete to raise money in October of 2000 and I ran a clay shoot. A steam organ provided fairground music, which got all the young kids dancing round it".* In succeeding years the October event increased in size and complexity too. At first, it housed a medieval reenactment society under the guise of Oak Apple Day, before becoming firmly established as a Working Steam Weekend, celebrating the steam-driven machines which had revolutionised 19th century agriculture. The October weekend remains a more low-key and traditional event, greatly enjoyed by both volunteers and visitors. Amongst the favourite attractions is the opportunity to watch corn being threshed by a steam-driven machine, before being taken to the Mill by horse and cart to be ground into flour – and then buying the end product.

Chapter Fifteen

By the 2001 May Open Day, the shell of the Mill building was up and the ground floor open. That year, Jan Radford provided tea in Stotfoldbury's paddock with shelter provided by tents borrowed from the Stotfold Scouts group. The attractions and stalls had expanded: while there were still cakes, bric-a-brac, souvenirs, plants and books, there were also hand-made cards; turned wood items by George Arnold, using timber salvaged from the Mill; displays of stationary steam engines, tractors and motorbikes; working model ships and steam engines; classic cars, plus a few traction engines; the famous duck race; Shire horses; a beer tent and a pig roast.

Jan has continued her involvement with feeding the hungry volunteers over the years. She explained, *"I started with a camping stove and was delighted when we progressed to a proper hot-plate. I always think the Staff Tent is the hub of the Show. Everyone comes there in their free time, to tell each other what's been happening in their area. We love sending them back refreshed for their next stint. They all seem to enjoy the food and it is very rewarding to hear the comments as they leave."*

Trev Radford spoke of the hard work running this event entailed. *"I remember walking home one time so exhausted I could hardly put one foot in front of the other, but it was worth it to see thousands of people turning up to support us. There were so many people who gave up so much time to make these events a success and still do. Not just the three or four days I might put in to the May weekend, but hundreds of hours."*

It was quickly realised that in order to raise significant funds, there would need to be a specialist team organising the May weekend. John Hyde said, *"Christine Smith asked if I was interested in expanding the event to something much bigger, so with John Saunders' steam*

Piling corn into the thesher (left) before the grain is lifted into the luccam

gear and Christine's experience from her work at Knebworth, in 2002 we set up the first Steam Fair. Christine, Mary Pateman and I did everything from road closure to organising the formal Mill Ball."

Mary Pateman remembered, *"The first meeting of the new Events Team was held at my house. I didn't know most of the people but they were already heavily involved and with fantastic experience. We had no idea how big the Steam Fair would get. If I'm honest I didn't have a clue. We were lucky that Christine knew how to do this from her experience at Knebworth. The Events Team at first was three people all through the winter, me, John Hyde and Christine, plus Jan Osborn and Simon Barrow. We later met once a week at Christine's house with different ideas and discussed how many people would be needed.*

My job was to muster the troops. Christine dealt with business; John Hyde did setting up. The idea was John Saunders would bring a few steam engines and we would have a few stalls to raise money. If I'd had any idea of how big this would get I'd have been too scared to do it. The first year was wonderful, well-supported by the community." She added, *"I've made fantastic friends I would never have met otherwise without my involvement with the Mill. The passion and the pride is the same for everyone. It's the future we're giving our children."*

John Saunders' internationally famous steam collection has become an integral part of the Steam Fair and Country Show. John said, *"I*

A steam lorry in front of the Mill

Chapter Fifteen

Steam yachts delighting visitors

inherited my interest in steam from my father who had been fascinated by it since he was a boy. When he was quite young as part of the parade for Stotfold Hospital Day he went round with a small truck with a boiler and a chimney with real smoke, that he had made himself. I remember the first steam machine he bought when I was eleven. It was a steam roller – a Fowler from Kitchener's of Potton. He really wanted a showman's engine, but he couldn't afford it at the time. That was the start of the Saunders Collection, which is now one of the biggest in Europe, if not the world. He restored the steam roller on site, put in new tubes etc and then drove it home, up Vaughan Road at tea time. The machine set people's tea cups rattling, so they all came out to see what was passing."

John continued, *"I brought a few steam engines to the first Steam Fair, and keep being amazed how it's grown to what it is today. When I was a kid people from all the local villages used to come to the Stotfold Feast; now they come for the Steam Fair. You can see the strength of support of the whole community."* He added, *"I support the Mill as it's part of my family, my history, my core as a Stotfold person and I believe charity begins at home. The Steam Collection is invited to Holland, Germany, Finland as well as all over the UK but out of all the places, we travel to, the Stotfold Steam Fair is special because the Mill is at the centre. It's unique because you see the whole process from steam*

Local Fundraising And Major Events

ploughs to threshing to watching the corn being ground into flour."

As it was realised that the event would only increase in size and complexity, the small group of original volunteers expanded into the Major Events Team who work to ensure successful operation of both the May Steam Fair and the October event. They came up with the ideas for the publicity programmes and for funding them by selling advertising. John Hyde suggested Jan Osborn would be ideal to organise the advertising sales, which, despite ill health, she was still doing in 2012.

Jan said, *"My father was a local newsagent and we knew about the Mill from childhood. At the beginning I used to count the money at the May Fairs and went on to join the Events Committee and sell advertising in the programmes. I did this over the phone, first to local business people I knew. It was small-scale at the start, but like Topsy, it grew and grew. I think one of the great highlights for me has been the Duke of Edinburgh's visit. I'm so proud that the Mill has become such a big part of the community and that it is something so lovely for the village."*

Christine Smith explained, *"The Major Event Meetings were held in my dining room while the Mill was still being restored. We got better every year. I remember the first Steam Fair poster was a photograph of the back of the Mill, taken by John Hyde, from a rowing boat on the river."*

She added, *"The first year we had a main marquee which held the Craft Stalls and which then hosted the Mill Ball in the evening. That year was very wet, so most of the men were hosing mud from the road outside the Mill on the night. We held May Balls for two to three years and had live music, caterers and a bar. On a sunny evening it was great to see people in DJs and long dresses walking through the village to the marquee."*

The Mill Ball was originally held on the Saturday of the May Steam Fair, but it added significantly to the already huge demands made of the Major Events Team and many of the volunteers found they were so worn out after the day's work that they did not fully enjoy the evening. The Ball was eventually moved to a separate date and then discontinued as it actually yielded small profits for all the work and costs involved in its organisation.

However, the Steam Fairs developed rapidly as Christine Smith recalled, *"The second year we had a separate marquee for crafts and the community stalls evolved. Then we added arena events and traders. Originally all were in the first meadow and then we expanded, with a dedicated car park on Millennium Green. I am proud that it has stood the test of time and become popular, not just in the local community,*

Chapter Fifteen

A historic horse-drawn fire engine adds to the fun of the Steam Fair

but further afield. It's a lovely day of old-fashioned fun. To be able to maintain that is what is most pleasing."

Organisation for the Steam Fair and Country Show, always held on the first weekend after the May Bank Holiday, starts early, as Mary Pateman related. *"Once you get past Christmas the first letter goes out with plans for the next year. The Events Team meet every one or two weeks from then. At the beginning I'd have to organise the volunteer passes and confirm jobs to everyone in person as this was before most people had email. Delivering the leaflets publicising the Steam Fair was a great way to lose weight. The third year the dog and I walked and delivered to the whole of Stotfold."*

She added, *"A lot of people wanted to help but couldn't do physical stuff, so they made cakes or sent donations. There were different levels of support and everyone was welcomed. I am nostalgic about the early days as they were simpler."* Even when Mary stopped formally working on the Major Events Team, she carried on as a member of the Car Parking and Marshalling Teams, which as she confessed, *"in my case means working all weekend in May and October."*

As well as organisational work starting early, the practical arrangements for the weekends begin well before the first member of the public appears. Robert Smith emphasised the importance of the Set-up Team, led by John Hyde and Simon Barrow, which starts work on Friday. He added, *"I'm also part of the team which organises road closures, together with Geoff Osborn and Richard Whitelock and we start at 7 am each day of the Steam Fair."*

John Hyde also recruited Kevin Balderstone, who joined the Team in 2004, taking on the role of looking after the Health and Safety aspects of the event. The steam engines had become a major attraction so Kevin, as Safety Officer, ensured the event was run in accordance with the National Traction Engine Trust (NTET) code of practice for steam rallies. When Tim Naisbitt stood down in 2011, Kevin also took on the role of Event Chairman.

Simon Barrow, another member of the team recruited by John Hyde, said, *"I had no experience of show organising, but had been to a lot of other country shows, so for me it was easy – just make our show what I wanted to see if I was out for the day myself. It had to be interesting, varied and sensibly-priced – something we still strive to achieve today.* He added, *"It was quite easy in the early days. We would chat about the show and content and vote on it with a simple yes/no, but as it has got more successful and bigger all sorts of new problems have come into play, from health and safety issues, insurance, traffic, road closures and so on. The list is endless."*

Simon went on, *"I am very proud of what we as a group of inexperienced volunteers have achieved over the last ten years. I like to think we put on a very well-run show; that's not to say there aren't any problems, but luckily we always manage to get around them."*

Kara Buchan became involved with organising the Steam Fair in 2002. She had been a trader for 30 years with lots of involvement with farmers' markets, steam fairs and craft fairs, so was approached by Mary Pateman and Christine Smith to organise the Craft Marquee. She commented, *"I always work with Simon Barrow on the site plan and contact and co-ordinate all the traders who make the Craft Marquee so attractive to visitors. I love the stress, the anguish, the hours spent on the phone. Seriously, I am very proud to have been part of the Major Events Team and to see the events grow immensely over the years."*

Geoff Osborn organises the ticket money and entrance gates for the fundraising weekends, as well as managing security. He commented, "Though I lived in Letchworth I was always in Stotfold because I had friends here, who I got to know at the swimming pool in Letchworth. Sam was always happy to show us kids round the Mill. If you were interested he could be really friendly; a lovely man who was keen to show how the Mill worked and to talk about the old days in Stotfold. He could be blunt, though. When the Mill first opened, Sam was really amused that we had toilets. When I asked him what he used to do, the response was 'Out of the window, Geoff'."

I moved to Stotfold when I married my wife, Jan, and over the years I was kept up to date with snippets of information from John Hyde and others. When they started the first Steam Fair, John asked me to join the Events Committee, but I didn't have any spare time because of my building business, so Jan joined instead. By the time of the fifth Show, Jan's Multiple Sclerosis had got worse. She couldn't carry on with the Committee, so I took her place. Jan added, *"Though I'm not*

Chapter Fifteen

formally on the Committee now, I still help with selling advertising and whatever else I can."

Geoff radically changed the organisation of the entrance gates *"from a table with a box for the money, to proper cabins for ticket collectors."* He also came up with the idea of bridging the river so people could enter the fields directly from the car park, as well as from in front of the Mill. Geoff works at both the Steam Fair and Country Show and the Working Steam Weekend and he and his son Chris also help with the set up on the days before the event. He commented, *"I do it because I believe in the Mill. It's a focal point for Stotfold; it's Stotfold's identity and our gateway to the future. Very few places are lucky enough to have a working mill. It really brings people together."*

Pam Peacock described her main tasks as *"liaising with local schools, community groups and charities and sorting out the bands."* She first got involved with the Mill in 2005 *"as Jonathan Ellis thought my skills would be good to use on the Major Events Team."* She added, *"I love working with people and you definitely get to meet all sorts by volunteering. The Mill holds a special place in my heart as I live so close to it and if I can give something back and help it to continue, I will. There are so many highlights, but for me the main one has got to be meeting the Duke of Kent when he visited the Mill in 2011."*

Debbie Shepherd got involved as she knew Jan and Geoff Osborn. She started working on entrance gates in 2006 and then moved on

Volunteers at the entrance gates before visitors start arriving: Ilona Clifton and Saul Ackroyd chatting with Helen Muggeridge

Geoff Osborn and Alan Greenshields in front of the Mill entrance door

Local Fundraising And Major Events

to helping run the Staff Refreshment Tent, which is a vital part of the success of the weekend events. Tired and hungry volunteers are refreshed by tea, burgers, cakes or Jan Radford's now-famous bacon butties. Debbie commented, "*I enjoy it because you get to meet everyone involved with the event, including people you wouldn't meet normally. I also work with Kevin on Health and Safety, particularly food hygiene.*"

Robert Smith joined the Mill volunteers via his wife, Christine. He remembered, "*I started at the same time as Christine, not on the same committees, but mainly supervising car parking. In the first year we had 450 cars over two days, now we get that number in a couple of hours. We started with one field as a car park, but after a few years that was getting completely filled and we had to expand to the next field. Every year we learn more and get more professional. Now we have high visibility yellow jackets for all our team, radios to enable us to co-ordinate parking better and sensors to count the number of cars. The car parking team has a core who have stayed over the years. I'd love to be more involved in photographing the events but till I had people I could trust I couldn't do this. I can now. We all have a bit of a laugh together and usually end up at the finish near the cold beverages (aka beer) tent. From a team of four we're now fourteen and we don't stop all day. We have our own radio channel so we can share stories and have a debrief at the end. It's real team work.*"

Tim Naisbitt became part of the Major Events Team in 2009 and for

Car parkers taking a well-earned break after a hard day. L to R: Geoff Osborn, Ian and Keryl Rutherford, Robert Smith, Richard Whitelock, Mary Pateman, Paul Clifton

Chapter Fifteen

the next two years led the team in organising the Steam Fair and October Working Steam Weekend. Tim, who had recently moved to the town, found his involvement *"very challenging, but a good way to get to know people at the heart of Stotfold."* He added new attractions, including a bar selling real ales and a Farmers' Market, besides streamlining much of the organisation of the events.

Jonathan Ellis had volunteered to help with the Steam Fair from the beginning and was persuaded by John Hyde to join the organising group. He said, *"I initially focused on the commercial side of the event, looking to see where and how we could make the most revenue. I also got involved in helping with marketing and more recently I have worked on bar and food suppliers. Also I have been involved with the entertainment over the weekend, working with the team on the launch of our successful Live@The Mill rock music night and organising the local bands that play over the weekend."* The rock concert premièred in 2012 and was so successful that it is planned to continue this in future years.

Jonathan continued, *"The highlight for me is working with such a committed and enthusiastic team of volunteers, always looking for ways to improve the event and coming up with new ideas."* He added, *"It is nice to put something back into the community."*

2012 was a special year for the Events Committee as it marked the tenth anniversary of the Steam Fairs, but it was nearly a disaster. Simon Barrow commented, *"2012 was, unfortunately, the wettest year on record. With shows being cancelled in the week leading up to our show, many of us were keeping a very close eye on the weather forecasts. Right up till the week of the show, it was a bit iffy. The rain should have stopped on Thursday morning but the downpour at dinner time*

Volunteers being thanked by Kevin Balderstone, on behalf of the Trustees, for all their hard work at the 2012 Steam Fair

Local Fundraising And Major Events

nearly finished us off; vehicles were getting stuck and needed pulling on site and the show ground was getting very chewed up, which was not good for health and safety. However, we hung on, the sun came out and eventually we got around the problems and delivered a very successful show with a record crowd."

Christmas comes to Stotfold Watermill

The Major Events year is rounded off by the now-famous Santa at the Mill weekend run by Julie Hyde. This event underlines the community element of the Mill and the creative decorations transform the building, delighting visitors of all ages. The highlight of each child's visit is the chance to talk with Father Christmas in his grotto and receive a small gift.

Julie said, *"I started organising this five or six years ago because I love Christmas. We started in The Barn, my business premises, doing the event as a gift to the village. Then as it got bigger we moved to the Mill. We still don't charge admission, but ask for a donation, so it's a bonus if we raise money. There was nothing happening for kids when we started, but now lots of people have jumped on the bandwagon."*

She explained, *"I do all the construction and preparation, with Ray Kilby and my husband, John. Themes are run for a couple of years as it is a lot of work to devise and set up. For 2012 we had a Willie Wonka theme which really tested us. It takes us about two weeks and without the help of the girls from The Barn I just couldn't do it. The shop sponsored all the presents from Santa at the beginning but now we get additional sponsors. We used to get 50-100 children; last year we got 500 plus. We can't get any bigger because we're limited for space in the Mill."* She added, *"I do love meeting the young families and seeing the children's little faces light up. It puts some value back into Christmas and means it's not all about big presents, it's fun for children and a real community event."*

MAJOR EVENTS TEAM 2012:

Leader: *Kevin Balderstone*

Steering Group Members: *Simon Barrow; Kara Buchan; Jonathan Ellis; John Hyde; Geoff Osborn; Jan Osborn; Pam Peacock; Debbie Shepherd; Christine Smith; Robert Smith, plus up to 150 volunteers for each Major Event weekend.*

CHAPTER SIXTEEN

MARKETING AND SMALL EVENTS TEAMS

Doug Pearson had been thinking about early retirement and was considering working with a local charity. After looking at various organisations within a five mile radius of Stotfold he had begun to decide that,"*the Mill seemed a good option. Then, while cycling back from the bank in 2007, Paul Redwood nearly knocked me off my bike and we got talking.*" They had previously worked for the same company and, following his conversation with Paul, Doug joined the Sustainable Development Committee, linked to the Marketing Team, which had been searching for volunteers with business development skills. Money had been relatively easy to raise for the rebuild but ongoing funding was a problem as the Mill and Nature Reserve need a revenue stream of approximately £23,000 every year.

It was clear that selling flour and income from the Shop and Tea Room could not expand significantly, so Doug and Paul Redwood proposed additional ways to raise funds, to try to ensure the Mill could become financially viable and secure, with relatively little effort and no need for a huge increase in volunteer commitment. Ideas suggested included generating hydropower from the river, hiring out the Ivel Room and holding functions there and expanding existing business lines. The group also discussed the importance of succession planning – recruiting more young volunteers to ensure future sustainability.

Doug commented, "*The major proposal was to pick six ideas we really knew we could do and which would add value. I am really proud that we made people realise that everything was dependent on volunteers.*" He added, "*Getting people to think about the Boston Square – examining strengths, weaknesses, opportunities and threats – was a real epiphany as it shows that you can't have events or plans that take a lot of people and bring in little money. You need to concentrate on what you can do with the fewest people and for the greatest result in money terms.*"

Though Doug ceased his involvement with the Marketing Team, he has continued to be a lynch pin at the Major Events, as well as working as a guide to visitors. He said, *"I really enjoy setting up events, as it's very hands-on and completely different to what I did at work. I love seeing a bare field transformed into a vibrant and welcoming place."*

After Paul Redwood's health forced him to reduce his involvement with the Mill, Christine Smith took over this team. The focus has changed, though it is intended that a specialist Sustainable Development Team will be re-formed in the near future.

Christine who grew up in Letchworth, later lived in Canada and Arlesey, before finally moving to Stotfold in the 1980s when she married Robert. She started her involvement with the Mill in 2001, after attending a meeting asking for volunteers. She first joined the Events Team, which she chaired for seven years, as well as organising marketing of the Mill. In 2011, realising that marketing was key to the Mill's success, Christine recruited several volunteers to help in promoting the Mill and Nature Reserve as a visitor attraction. Christine's work at nearby Knebworth House, provides *"a good background to work from, with good training about spotting ideas and deciding what is achievable and what is not."*

Christine commented, *"Because of my employment experience, I was in charge of publicity from the beginning. The first few years of publicity for the Steam Fair were very basic. We did a lot of it ourselves as there was no money for graphic designers. My brother-in-law did a lot of work for us for free. Once we opened officially I was more involved in the visitor experience (though I hate that phrase). Lots of things have proved successful. I've particularly enjoyed seeing things develop from the beginning, including the marketing and seeing the Mill become well-known and a great focus for the community. We are developing the continual use of the Mill during the months of opening, so there is usually something happening on open Sundays from March to October. Ultimately I would like to open more often but that is restricted because of the limitations in numbers of volunteers."*

The first information leaflets were produced in 2008 and this venture has been very successful in attracting visitors to the Mill and Nature Reserve. The 25,000 leaflets printed in 2012 were distributed to every home in Stotfold, and to numerous outlets across Bedfordshire and Hertfordshire, as well as Tourist Information Centres. The attractive publication lists the growing programme of activities and exhibitions hosted by the Mill, as well as details of the history, restoration, and visitor attractions, including the Tea Room, Shop and Nature Reserve. In 2012 the Mill held 27 open days and had over 6,500 visitors, including many from increasingly further afield.

Chapter Sixteen

Christine Smith also proposed that the Mill needed its own guidebook, so in 2009 an editorial team comprised of Pat Clarey, Pam Manfield, Trevor Radford and Christine set to work to produce one. Besides details of the history and restoration, the creation of the Nature Reserve and explanations of the milling equipment and process, this included meticulous line drawings by Geoff Hoile and striking photographs, including the cover, by Robert Smith, seen also on the cover of this book.

Robert commented, *"I am proud that my photo of the back of the Mill has become a classic and is on all the leaflets and the guidebook. I've been interested in photography since I was 14 and am self-taught. I have also got involved with recording some of the historical work being done at the Mill. When they last changed the millstones I took 150 pictures over two days. It's good that you can change the lighting when the Mill is closed as you get better quality photos. Cameras have got better over the years too but you still have to be in the right place, at the right time, for that special image. It's nice to be able to use photography to a good end."*

At the end of 2012, the Marketing Team took over responsibility for the website, following a decision by the Trustees to invest in a redesign. In addition to the website, from 2012 the Mill also ran a Facebook page. Cara Downey and Emma Whiteway help with the postings and Lucy Clarke's computer graphic skills provide imaginative posters advertising Mill events and activities.

Funds raised at the 2012 Steam Fair and Country Show also enabled an investment in producing information panels to further enhance visitors' enjoyment of the Mill and Nature Reserve. Several panels give a brief overview of the history of the Mill, the 1992 fire and subsequent rebuild, while others display details about the Nature Reserve, the work of volunteers and the Education Programme.

In 2011, Christine started a programme of events and exhibitions in the Mill, which were included in the promotional leaflet.

One of the new display panels, encouraging volunteer involvement

Marketing And Small Events Teams

(Left) Magical Midsummer Music by the Hitchin Symphony Orchestra (below) Roy Figgis and his wife relate the story of candles through the ages

The programme proved popular and expanded so much that a Small Events Team was set up at the end of 2012, under the leadership of Jean Kersey, to assist the Marketing and Millers Wheel Teams. Primarily they would plan an interesting programme of events and exhibitions to attract additional visitors to the Mill and also to raise funds.

The group came up with ideas for a highly varied programme for 2013, including a microwave cookery demonstration; the Miller's Tale – a night time tour of the Mill with stories and anecdotes with a milling background, as part of National Museums at Night Week; a concert by the Hitchin Symphony Orchestra; a Bedfordshire folk song evening; the Great Stotfold Bake-off; a children's night at the Mill; a gourmet cheese and salami tasting event and a carols and mulled wine evening.

Special emphasis was placed on activities for children, including a short story writing competition. A variety of themed craft workshops, led by Jean Kersey, ranged from Easter crafts to bugs and butterflies; the seaside; princesses and pirates and Christmas crafts. Jean stated, *"I enjoy crafts and spend a lot of time making things with my grandchildren, so I offered to run the Krafty Kids sessions during the school holidays. These have proved great fun – if very messy."*

Chapter Sixteen

Afternoon activities included a special programme by the Letchworth and District Gardeners' Association with a history of gardening and a panel of experts to solve vegetable growing problems; a guide to orchid growing by a local expert, plus showings of rare and newly-discovered videos of the Mill restoration. Special exhibitions were put on by the Mill's Archive Team, with much of the display material coming from the Mill's own documents. The 2013 programme included Wartime Memories; Secrets of the Mill Archives and Meet the Randalls – the story of the family who ran the Mill for a hundred years.

MARKETING TEAM 2012:

Leader: Christine Smith

Team Members: Lucy Clarke, Cara Downey, Margaret Griffiths, Jean Kersey, Pam Manfield and Emma Whiteway

SMALL EVENTS TEAM 2012:

Leader: Jean Kersey

Team Members: Saul Ackroyd; Linda Brown; Lisa Lyons; Pam Manfield; Nicky McIver; Lindsay Ray; Emma Whiteway; Hilary Woods

CHAPTER SEVENTEEN

THE MILLING AND MAINTENANCE TEAM

2006 was a landmark date for Stotfold Watermill, as it was the first time the restored millstones produced flour. Ron Roper, who had wanted to run the Mill as a working business, led the team on that momentous occasion. The first flour was, as Ray Kilby confessed, *"rather gritty"* as the setup of the stones and grain feed needed some fine tuning. In the early days, as most of the millers had not followed the traditional path of a long apprenticeship, they were learning as they went along. Since then, the team have honed their skills and Stotfold Watermill's stone-ground flour has become famous locally for its taste and quality.

Ray Kilby, who now is the most frequent miller, said, *"Before Ron moved to Norfolk, he trained a few people to work the Mill – Phil Radford, me, Patrick Chalmers and Peter James. After that I trained John Hyde and Tim Wells. Currently we have two trainees – Simon Law and Glenn Rodford. You really only understand machinery by keeping using it and seeing how it operates, but since we only mill on Sundays from March to October when the Mill is open it is difficult for people to get enough experience, to understand what has happened if the machines suddenly stop, for example."*

Ron Roper and Phil Radford discussing flour production

The milling process starts when the threshed grain is delivered to the Mill. Traditionally, this would have been raised by hoist through the luccam and this is still done at the Steam Fair and Working Steam weekends, as a demonstration. However, generally the grain is now loaded into the lift and

Chapter Seventeen

taken to the Dressing Floor, where it is then raised via the sack hoist to the Secret Floor for storage.

Ray Kilby commented, *"We always try to source local grain. In 2012 this was Cordiale, produced by Tim Kitchener at Astwick. It's a hard wheat, ideal for bread making. In 2013 we will be using Gallant from Northerns at Radwell, which has the same qualities.*

When we start milling the first bag goes through the bolter to settle the stones as they can be variable as they start up. Phil and I have sorted this, so it runs at the right speed with the right mesh to reduce the bran percentage to 18%, which is really good. If the stones are not dressed correctly – not sharp – they don't allow air through to keep the flour cool. Before stones are dressed the edge can be dulled and the flour heats up, which can kill it. It takes all the nutrients out and liberates the gluten. Then when it goes through the bolter, the gluten sticks to the sieve. It is really important to feel the temperature of the flour; if you try to get the flour too fine, you can tell by the smell of burning."

The grain is cleaned in the winnower and then moves via a chute down to the hopper above the millstones. The hopper is supported by the horse, which is part of the wooden frame or furniture surrounding the stones. The shoe channels grain through the top of the tun into the hole at the centre of the millstones. A shutter on the front of the hopper regulates the flow of grain into the shoe. The miller can control the amount of grain falling into the eye, the centre gap in the millstone, by raising and lowering the shoe from the floor below, by using the crook string.

The damsel – the raised metal bar at the centre of the stone – which sits on top of the mace (or millrynd) consists of four small metal rods. As it rotates the damsel agitates the shoe, pushing it from side to side against the spring of a willow stick – known as the miller's wand. This sends grain steadily into the eye of the runner stone. This is the top stone and as the name suggests, the stone which rotates.

It is essential that the flow of grain between the stones is maintained whenever the machinery is running, as the stone faces need to be continually lubricated to minimise friction. Flour dust is reputedly 40 times more flammable than coal dust, so every effort has always been taken in traditional mills to minimise this hazard. There is a leather band inside the hopper, which is normally out of sight under the grain. If the level of grain falls beneath the band, it rises and releases the bell arm. The ringing of the bell alerts the miller, who is usually working on another floor. He then has time to ensure that more grain is released into the hopper and hence onto the stones, so preventing a dangerous build up of heat. 'Keeping your nose to the grindstone' is an ancient saying, based on the need for the apprentice millers to be constantly ready to detect any smell of burning.

Ray Kilby explained how a good miller needs to use all his senses, besides just watching what is happening. *"You have to listen to the stones because they talk to you – and can grumble as well,"* he said. *"The best speed is 60-80 revolutions per minute (rpm). At first you need to count to check the speed, but after a while you just know when they're working correctly. You also need to use your sense of touch, to feel the flour and check its consistency. You can smell if the stones are burning, so you're using all your senses all the time.*

We need only 1.5 inches of water above the shelf over the waterwheel to run the machines. That gives us four horse power. To run the stones and grind flour we need another six horse power, so that's 4-6 inches above the shelf. The water level is regulated by paddles, operated by the miller. Once the machinery is running, we lower the stone to create the type of flour we need to produce. The faster they move, the more flour we make. We reduce the water level by dropping the sluice so we can run at 65 rpm which is the best speed for the French Burr stones". The huge machinery can stop surprisingly quickly, as Ray explained, *"We can turn the water off by dropping the sluice via a wheel near the pitwheel. It will stop in just 5-6 seconds."*

John Dunn examing the stone furniture

Chapter Seventeen

The millstones are encased by the tun, which is airtight in the same way as a beer barrel, so that the flour thrown out from the edges of the stones does not escape. The flour drops down a hole beside the lower, stationary, bedstone through a chute to the floor below where it is collected into sacks. These are then raised by the sack hoist through the trapdoors of the two lower floors to the Secret Floor.

The stones first produce wholemeal flour. If white flour is needed it is sieved in the bolter, which is a fine canvas sieve revolving inside a wooden cabinet. The finer white flour drops through the sieve while the bran is collected at the end.

Ray explained how everything needs to be checked carefully before any milling begins. *"We make sure we have the bins set up and full of grain, the chutes open, there is grain already in the hopper and the "rat-traps" have been removed. The traps actually stop damp, moths and insects getting in. On the hursting floor we put a flour sack at the bottom of the chute and then start the stones. If you forget to take off the trap, no grain gets to the stones, it spreads everywhere and you get a rumbling sound and smell of burning. You have to turn the water off fast, to stop everything.*

You need a routine to start everything up, with a clear sequence so you can check you have covered everything every time. The stones weigh three quarters of a ton each, so if things are not done properly they could

Relaxing after work on the millstones: John Dunn, Ray Kilby, Phil Radford and Neil Medcalf

The Milling And Maintenance Team

really create a safety issue. Stone dressing gauges are vital, especially for the concave runner stone. George and Sam have different profiles, so you need special gauges for each."

Stotfold Watermill produces wholemeal and white flour, as well as bran, as direct results of the milling process. Stoneground flour is widely recognised as superior to that produced in modern roller mills since, rather than being crushed, the grain is sliced, increasingly finely and less heat is generated in the process. This retains more of the basic goodness of the wheat. Oats have also become a popular item and the restored oat crusher on the Dressing Floor is in regular production.

For the two major fundraising weekends, Ron Roper, who was so deeply involved in the restoration of the Mill, returns from his home in Norfolk to Stotfold. He puts on his trademark embroidered miller's smock and once again helps to produce flour, while wife Lynn helps with flour sales to visitors.

Throughout the year, whether the Mill is open to the public or not, there is a vast amount of work going on in the background to ensure that the Mill machinery and building remain in excellent condition and all is ready for the new season. Grain is delivered and cleaned.

Ron Roper, in traditional miller's smock, with Glenn Rodford, explaining the milling process to a visitor

Both sets of stones are opened, cleaned and reinstalled so they are ready to begin grinding again. Ray Kilby said, "*We used to clean all the grain in the winter, but we are going to start doing this on open Sundays also, so the visitors can watch what happens."*

He added, "*We clean and regrease all the wooden teeth, all the wheels, the wallower and the stone nuts. All old grease is taken off and replaced with tallow – animal fat mixed with vegetable oil to make it pliable. We melt it and paint it on. There are a hell of a lot of teeth to cover – over 400.*

I also put tack on the belts, which makes them slightly sticky so they grip the pulleys, and also clean the chutes. There's a lot of trial and error in getting the machinery working properly. It took some time to work out that the optimum inclination for the chutes is 25 degrees as if it's lower the grain will not run."

John Hyde, who rebuilt the Mill and stayed on as Trustee, also has a practical involvement in renovating and repairing the building. In 2012 this included the major task of repainting the outside of the Mill, in the traditional cream colour.

Since the Mill is open to visitors from March to October, it is vital that the place is clean, tidy and welcoming and Richard Whitelock has taken an important role in overseeing this, as well as fulfilling his role in the Milling and Archive Teams. Mick Barrow also does several of the background jobs, without which the Mill could not function. Mick first became involved when his wife, Julia, was asked to develop and then manage Randalls Tea Room. As Julia commented, "*All the shopping was done with Mick's help; I couldn't have done it without him.*" Although Julia has had to step out of her involvement with Randalls, Mick has continued to look after the Mill garden, behind the Tea Room, cutting the lawn and putting in bedding plants, ensuring bins are emptied regularly and also helping keep the river clear of debris. He also still helps out at Major Events, together with his son, Simon.

Mick is one of the few volunteers with a direct link to the history of the Mill, as he is a descendant of William Sarl, who was foreman miller to the young John Randall in the mid 19th century. He said of his involvement with the Mill, "*I enjoy it as people are so nice and I've made so many friends. I hope the seeds we sowed will be there for the next generation to enjoy. We have achieved a lot.*"

Milling and Maintenance Team 2012:

Leaders: John Hyde; Ray Kilby and Phillip Radford

Team Members: Mick Barrow; John Dunn; Simon Law; Trevor Radford; Glenn Rodford; Ron Roper; Richard Whitelock

CHAPTER EIGHTEEN

RANDALLS TEA ROOM

Randalls opened in April 2006 under the management of Julia Barrow, who ran it until health problems and family commitments forced her to leave in December 2009. The name was chosen in tribute to the Randall family who ran the Mill for several generations.

From the first, the emphasis was on creating a welcoming atmosphere for visitors, achieved by hanging paintings by Stotfold Art Group on the bare brick walls and having red tablecloths and posies of fresh flowers on each table. Windows overlooking the River Ivel and an outside boardwalk, which enables visitors to feed the local family of swans, all add to the attraction.

Julia and her husband Mick became involved as their son Simon was a regular helper with John Hyde in organising the set up of the May Steam Fair and Country Show, one of the major fund raising events. In 2004, Simon persuaded Julia to help raise funds by selling cakes from a stall in the meadow. Later that year she met with Robin Tasker and Paul Martin to give advice about the proposed Tea Room and in December was asked to take on setting up the project.

Julia was an excellent choice to manage the Tea Room as she had long experience in baking, having trained at Day's Bakery in Ashwell and worked for Tesco and for Allen's Bakery. From the start she did all the baking for the Mill and Randalls became famous for the quality of its cakes, with only gluten-free products being bought in. Eleven varieties of cakes were provided, though the favourite was always coffee and walnut. However, Julia remembered, *"One man from Letchworth used to love the fruit spice cake and would happily go away with a whole one every time he visited."* The menu quickly expanded to five types of scones, cream teas, and soups, with mulled wine and mince pies at the Christmas Weekend.

The Tea Room had a very limited budget at first, having to make do with a second-hand fridge-freezer and long rolls of red and white gingham plastic material cut to table cloth size, until they were able

Chapter Eighteen

Julia Barrow at work

to progress to proper tablecloths, handmade by Moira Batizorsky. Julia said, *"At first these were topped with paper sheets but later wipeable plastic cloths were used, which lasted longer."*

After Hartleys in Letchworth closed their shop, lots of crockery was donated to the Mill, originally intended for the China Smash stall at the May Event. When Julia investigated the *"boxes of stuff in the loft"* she found they included teapots, jugs, plates, water jugs and lots of cups. *"In the end we only had to buy some saucers, cutlery and flower vases. Hartleys saved us a lot of money,"* Julia commented. Rustic chairs for the new Tea Room came from the Salvation Army and John Saunders gave the tables.

Progress was slow and gradual and things were only bought as money became available, but from the beginning Julia wanted to have a quality feeling, with china cups and saucers and waitress service. *"Years ago I had visited Finchingfield near Saffron Walden which was set out perfectly, with clean linen and flowers and I used this as an example. It was always my ambition to have a Tea Room and this project gave it to me".* Gradually they were able to buy new fridge-freezers and a microwave, but *"it was make do and mend till we got going"* as Julia recalled.

The early volunteers were mainly the wives of those involved in clearing the debris, but as the Tea Room became more popular, adverts were placed locally, asking for extra help and Randalls now has a large group of dedicated helpers. One of the first of these was Sheila Archer, who recalled, *"I put my name on the volunteer list to wash up, but now I cover everything, including decorating the Tea Room for Christmas. If an idea is put forward and I think it's not right for the Mill, I say so. The new boiler was my idea; I thought the old one was dangerous. The Mill would be no good without the Tea Room. We're a good team who get on well and have a lot of fun".* Betty Miller was also involved at the beginning, especially helping with special events, like birthday parties, held in the Ivel Room.

Julia summed up her time at the Mill with quiet satisfaction. *"The real achievement was bringing it from nothing to 4 stars in the Food*

Hygiene awards in the very first year and building up our reputation so quickly. People came from a long way and would come again and bring groups to visit."

After Julia left, the Board of Trustees realised that running the Tea Room was a vital task, so Paul Redwood sent out a letter to all relevant volunteers asking if they were willing to take on the management role, either alone or as a group. Seven people came forward and agreed to run Randalls as a committee: Sheila Archer, Joan Cave, Andrea Fisher, Gill Foskett, Clare Kilby, Jean Prutton and Brenda Saunders. This group split the organisational work between them: Joan, Sheila and Jean ensure the tablecloths and tea towels are washed and ironed before each opening day or function and Joan and Sheila also provide and arrange the fresh flowers on each table. Gill organises the volunteer rotas, Clare does the ordering and arranges functions, as well as representing the Tea Room on the Mill Management Committee, while Brenda and Andrea cover wherever needed.

Joan Cave first became involved as she knew Chris Webster through their membership of a local choir. She said, *"I've got to know a lot of people and it's good. I like to be busy and involved. Although we're all volunteers we still feel it's important to get in on time and keep commitments. The social side for volunteers is a bonus. I was lucky enough to meet the Duke of Kent; I'd never have done that if I hadn't been a Mill volunteer. The Mill is very special and I hope it continues to flourish."*

Several of the Tea Room volunteers discussing tasks. L to R: Clare Kilby; Sarah Law, Mavis Lyon; Gill Foskett; Brenda Saunders

Chapter Eighteen

Andrea Fisher confessed, *"I first got involved with the Mill because my parents (Brian and Brenda Saunders) are volunteers. Mum suggested I might enjoy it and I've been helping now for over five years."* She added, *"I enjoy the atmosphere and the people that I work with in the tearoom. We have some really lovely customers too, which makes it all worthwhile. It's good to have compliments from people about how nice the Tea Room and the Mill are."*

Gill Foskett moved to Stotfold in 1990 from Buckingham, because of her husband, Chris's job and got involved with the Mill via Chris, who had taken on the role of Mill Treasurer. She explained, *"There is a Tea Room meeting in February each year before the Mill opens and rotas are handed out to volunteers with a deadline for return. I work out the most suitable dates for each volunteer and the committee fill in any gaps."*

She added, *"I enjoy the company. We all have a good laugh even at busy times and at the end of each day, sit down and chat over tea and cakes. It's a really good way to meet people. I'd never done anything like this before. I would say to anyone to give it a try. Occasionally people find they don't like it, but that's not many. The only disadvantage is the size of the Tea Room, but possibly we wouldn't be able to cope with anything bigger – and we would need even more volunteers.*

We start at 11 am and work till the Mill closes. Sometimes it can be slow and we only have 50 customers over the six hours. The optimum number of volunteers is seven per shift. The first operates from 12.30

Tea Room volunteers at the end of an afternoon shift. L to R: Mavis Lyon; Sheila Archer; Jean Prutton; Helen Muggeridge; Jean Hill; Brenda Saunders Clare Kilby

to 2.30 or 2 and the second shift takes over till the end. Two committee members will be on each shift.

There's also work on Saturday, laying the cloths, putting flowers in vases on each table, setting out the cakes so they're ready for the volunteers to cut on Sunday. We decide amongst ourselves who does what. It's a big bonus that some people really enjoy washing up!"

Clare Kilby also became a volunteer as her husband was so deeply involved in work at the Mill. She commented, "*Ray's down at the Mill every Sunday, so I may as well be there too. The first year the Tea Room opened for the May weekend, I went in as a customer. Julia Barrow said, "I heard a rumour you'd like to help. Come in tomorrow then"* – *and that was the start."*

She confessed, "*I haven't had real catering experience, except for cooking for 80 plus Cubs and Scouts at camp, so the Tea Room was a challenge to start as none of us had done anything like it before. But we've all clicked together and sort out the different jobs between us. We're all friends and that does help. At first it was a challenge sorting out the ordering, but worth it, because we get such nice comments. We did find it difficult at the start, working out prices and the amounts to buy. We're still learning ways to be economical and not over-buy."*

She added, "*I enjoy working in the Tea Room; it's got a really friendly atmosphere and new people always comment on this. We're all different characters and we're all volunteers with different skills and different time commitments, but we can sort out rotas to suit most people. Even if they can only give one hour twice a year, it all helps."*

Jean Prutton has lived in Stotfold all her life and from early childhood remembered seeing the Mill working. She said, "*It fascinated us as kids, watching the grain bags swinging from the luccam."* She continued, "*There was a craft display in the Ivel Room a few years ago and I put my name down to help in the Tea Room. Julia Barrow was just leaving as manager and apparently I marked a box saying I was prepared to be on the committee, not dreaming what that entailed. I do like the fact we are bringing the Mill to life. It's our heritage and needs to be looked after and explained in the best possible way. I'm always encouraging people to come and see it. It's wonderful to see it restored and brought back to life and so good to see it working again as we did when we were kids."*

Brenda Saunders first joined the Mill as a volunteer for the Steam Fair and Country Show, working in the Staff Refreshment Tent for the first year, before she moved to helping in Randalls. She said, "*It was a bit daunting when we took over, but we thought, 'Yes we can do this.' The Management Committee works well as we all get on together.*

Chapter Eighteen

We haven't made major changes, but as none of us is a professional baker, we did agree to order baked items from a quality local bakery."

Randalls Tea Room continues to operate to the extremely high standards set from the beginning, including reaching the highest Food Hygiene Award of 5 stars in 2011 and has become a vital part of every visit to the Mill; visitors regularly comment on the quality of the food and the friendliness of the service. The coffee and walnut cake remains a particular favourite and a 2012 Facebook review talked of the *"adorable ladies in the Tea Room"*.

Tea Room Management Group 2012: Sheila Archer; Joan Cave; Andrea Fisher; Gill Foskett; Clare Kilby; Jean Prutton; Brenda Saunders

Team Members: Sue Barry; Jean Bean; Maureen Brooks; Heather Chalmers; Lucy Clarke; Isabel Collier; Wendy Craig; Anne Marie Friend; Jean Hill; Eileen Hoile; Jean Kersey; Jane Kirk; Alice Law; Sarah Law; Mavis Lyon; Helen Muggeridge; Marianne Myhill; Sue Pelter; Olivia Ravenall; Joyce Redwood; Lindsay Reynolds; June Richardson; Keryle Rutherford; Joan Trulock; Joan Vernon; Christine Webster; Linda Wilding.

CHAPTER NINETEEN

STOTFOLD ART GROUP

Robin Tasker invited the local Art Group to exhibit at the first fundraising weekend for the Mill and they have gone on to showcase their work at this, and the October event, every year since. When the first display was set up in the Mill building the windows were still unfinished, with the gaps covered in sheets of plastic and the walls needing repairs. Carolyn Monaghan remembered, *"The end wall was a horrible crumbly thing, the plaster was always falling off when we put nails in"* and Sheila Archer added, *"We had to take everything down as soon as the event was over as everything got wet and the paper started warping. So, we only put things up on the morning of the event to get people in"*.

When Randalls Tea Room was to be opened in 2006, Paul Martin met with the Group and talked about the need for brightening the

Art works brightening the Tea Room walls

Chapter Nineteen

A close-up of some of the art works on sale

bare brick walls in the former Engine House. Since then paintings by members have been displayed throughout the open season and, as Sheila Archer commented, *"The Art Group really brings life to the Tea Room; the walls are so bare without the pictures"*. From the start it was held to be important to have a theme which fitted in with the Mill ambiance, so works concentrate on countryside and wildlife subjects. Twenty five percent of the profits from the sale of artworks goes to the Trust and Geoff Hoile estimated that by 2012 the group had raised over £1,500.

One of Geoff Hoile's pictures used on the Nature Reserve lecterns

Geoff Hoile joined the Group in 1993/4, having retired early from British Aerospace. The Self-Help Art Group had been run since the early 1980s by Mid Bedfordshire Council Adult Education who had provided a tutor, from time to time. By 2004, however, there was very little practical Council support, so the Art Group chose to become an independent co-operative and Geoff became the unofficial tutor to the members.

Geoff is a talented artist in various media, including oil, watercolour and pastels and provided the line drawings of the Mill equipment for the Mill Guide Book. The great advantage of line drawings is that emphasis can be given to particular sections; photographs do not usually produce fine enough detail, particularly where pieces of equipment are concerned. Geoff commented, *"I had been an aerospace engineer, and should really have taken up model ship building in retirement, but instead I started painting and that took over. I always pick the subject first and then decide which medium suits it best."*

Geoff's paintings are often commissioned as gifts to prestigious visitors. The Duke of Edinburgh was presented with a Hoile original when he formally opened the Mill in 2006, as was Baroness Young when she opened the Nature Reserve in June 2011 and the Duke of Kent who visited in November 2011.

He has provided oil paintings for several permanent displays in the Mill, including panels depicting milling and maintenance activities, as well as portraits of the last three generations of millers. In addition, he has produced vibrant illustrations for the lecterns in the Nature Reserve and other areas of conservation in Stotfold. Members of the Art Group are active in other volunteer roles, including staffing the Shop and Tea Room and helping with special events and the Mill archive.

Membership of the group has changed over the years of its involvement with the Mill and Nature Reserve. However, the following have contributed significantly to the charity from the sale of their paintings and other work: Sheila Archer; Malcolm Goater; Geoff Hoile; Barbara Hook; Michael Lincoln; Carolyn Monaghan; Jenny Musselwhite; John Rennie; Jenny Riley and Richard Whitelock.

CHAPTER TWENTY

AWARDS AND RECOGNITION

The quality of the restoration work at the Watermill, the successful creation of the Nature Reserve and the efforts to ensure future sustainability of both have attracted many awards and significant recognition over the years. The logos of these awards can be seen on the inside front cover.

In 2001 and 2003 Stotfold Watermill Preservation Trust won the Environmental Section of Vauxhall's Griffin Award presented annually to *'organisations which make an outstanding contribution to the community through the development of new or enhanced service or project within the following categories – Community Development, Environment or Safety and Security.'*

The Trust was a National Gold Award Winner in the environmental class of the Green Apple Civic Pride Awards, 2004. This award celebrates *'outstanding environmental performance by recognising and publicising companies, corporations and individuals who are making an effort to preserve and protect the environment for generations to come.'*

The highly-prestigious Plaque from the Mills Section of the Society for the Protection of Ancient Buildings (SPAB) was awarded in 2006, but as there had been a lot of publicity from the visit to the Mill of the Duke of Edinburgh that year, SPAB were asked to delay the presentation until 2007. The award was fittingly made by Alan Stoyel, who had done so much to aid the saving and rebuilding of the watermill.

An article in the Mills Section newsletter, number 46, of January 1991 by Vincent Pargeter gave the criteria and background to the award:

> *'For some time the Section Committee has felt that due recognition should be given to good examples of mill conservation and repair. Windmill Certificates have been awarded regularly since 1935, and the Watermill Certificates since 1979, but these are presented to people or groups, and do not necessarily apply to a particular mill.*

The idea of a plaque that could be fixed to mills which had received sympathetic treatment was considered to be worth investigating, and has resulted in the design illustrated. The original layout was drawn by Tony Harcombe, an authority on stationary engines, and this has been modified slightly to take account of suggestions from members. The plaques, which are 9" by 7" will be cast in brass or bronze, and may be fastened outside or inside the building as deemed appropriate by the recipient.

The main criteria for this award will be as follows:

1. *How closely the repair work accords with the Wind and Watermill Section Philosophy of repair, paragraphs 5-8.*
2. *The standard of workmanship achieved.*

The following will also be taken into account:

1. *The extent to which interested local people and other enthusiasts have participated in the repairs, especially as this interest has acted as a stimulus for other repair work;*
2. *The resources of finance and manpower available to the organisers of the repair work.*
3. *A repair achieved under difficult circumstances .*
4. *The arrangements made for ongoing maintenance and the long-term future of the mill.*
5. *Any other special circumstances which make the repair work of particular interest.*

It is hoped that the plaques will show the Section's appreciation of repairs well done, and will serve to stimulate competition for high standards of workmanship in the conservation of our mills.'

Stotfold Watermill was only the fifth watermill to have been awarded this plaque, a real tribute to the excellence of craftsmanship involved in the restoration.

In addition to formal awards, there were also visits by distinguished visitors, recognising the Mill's status as an historic asset to the area. On 17th November 2006, HRH The Duke of Edinburgh visited the Mill to declare it formally open and to unveil a bronze statue of Sam Randall – 'The Last Miller' – by celebrated sculptor, John Mills. John Street recalled that one of the highlights of his involvement in the project was the Duke's visit – *"realising that the Mill had achieved something really worthwhile that had captured the attention of people in high places. It had given Stotfold a real shot in the arm."*

Chapter Twenty

The Duke of Edinburgh unveils the bronze of 'The Last Miller' at the formal opening of the Mill in 2006

The Bedfordshire section of the Campaign to Protect Rural England honoured Stotfold Watermill with its highest Living Countryside Award for landscape improvement in the Mill Meadows, at a presentation in Milton Ernest in 2009. Louden Masterton of Teasel and Paul Redwood of Stotfold Watermill were presented with the Gold Mark plaque by the BBC presenter Nicholas Crane, Vice-President of CPRE and well-known to millions of viewers as the man with the umbrella in his rucksack, from the television programme 'Coast'.

A CPRE spokesperson said, *"The CPRE Bedfordshire Living Countryside Awards scheme aims to recognise landowners, individuals and commercial users of the land who are making special efforts to preserve and enhance the visual appearance and biodiversity of Bedfordshire and to make a living from the countryside. Some of them receive little appreciation for their efforts to keep the landscape in good order for future generations; the awards seek to redress this and celebrate their achievements."*

Judges of the awards were all experts in recognising the unique value of the rural heritage of England: Matthew O'Brien, Countryside Advisor and representative for Bedfordshire's Farming and Wildlife Advisory Group (FWAG); Professor Jane Rickson, Chair in Soil Erosion and Conservation at Cranfield University and Steve Halton, Senior Project Officer – Community Partnerships with Central Bedfordshire Council.

Awards And Recognition

Ron Roper receiving the Queen's Award for Voluntary Service from the Lord Lieutenant of Bedfordshire, Sir Samuel Whitbread KCVO. (Right) The QAVS display in the Mill. (Below) Early volunteers, including most of the original group of 13 with the QAVS crystal. L to R: Trev Radford; Lynn Roper; Ron Roper; Jan Radford; Lorelie Tasker; Phil Radford; Frances Huckle; Louden Masterton; Geraldine Masterton; Patrick Chalmers; Jackie Radford.

Chapter Twenty

Stotfold Mill Meadows gained the award for its excellent planning over several years; its environmental protection; biodiversity; community access and involvement, including the 'Adopt a Tree' scheme. It was particularly commended as it is sponsored by local people and has good volunteer connections with the restored Mill.

In 2010 the Trust was awarded the Queen's Award for Voluntary Service, the MBE for voluntary groups, in recognition of the immense work of its volunteers in restoring and sustaining the Mill. On 30th July, Sir Samuel Whitbread, KCVO, Lord Lieutenant of Bedfordshire, representing Her Majesty the Queen, fittingly presented the award to Ron Roper, on behalf of all the volunteers.

Accepting the award Ron said, *"I am delighted to receive this prestigious award on behalf of all those involved in the restoration and continuing sustainability of Stotfold Watermill. Thousands of hours of volunteer time have resulted in the fully-functioning Mill you see today and it is wonderful to see all this hard work being recognised."*

The Campaign to Protect Rural England also awarded their highest honour – the CPRE Mark – to the Mill in 2010. The award was presented by Tony Juniper (on behalf of CPRE) to Paul Redwood and Christine Smith at a ceremony held at Howbury Hall, Renhold. Tony Juniper was Special Adviser to the Prince of Wales' Charities' International Sustainability Unit and, in partnership with His Royal Highness, wrote *'Harmony – a new way of looking at the world'*, intended to be a blueprint for a more balanced and sustainable world, blending ecology, biology and philosophy.

Christine Smith and Paul Redwood receiving the CPRE award from Tony Juniper

Awards And Recognition

The judges of the award – Professor Jane Rickson of Cranfield University; Steve Halton, Senior Project Officer: Ecology and Community at Central Bedfordshire Council and Nicolas Tye a renowned local architect – commented on the *"extensive, beautiful restoration of a Grade II listed building, with significant enhancement and protection of a historic landscape"* and the *"sympathetic and accurate restoration with attention to detail"*. They were particularly impressed by the educational value of the Mill and the extent of community involvement.

In 2010, following the evaluation and endorsement by Natural England, Central Bedfordshire Council awarded Local Nature Reserve status to the Mill Meadows in recognition of the enhancement of the natural landscape. The significant value of the area was further demonstrated in 2011 when Meadow Three was awarded County Wildlife Status, because of its importance as a habitat for rare and endangered water voles.

Stotfold Watermill Local Nature Reserve opened to the public on April 2nd, 2011, but was formally declared open on 5th June of that year by Baroness Young of Old Scone. She was an ideal choice, as her career has included being Chief Executive of the Royal Society for the Protection of Birds, Chair of English Nature and Chief Executive of the Environment Agency. She was created a Life Peer in 1997 in part for her sterling achievements in nature conservation.

Baroness Young opening the Nature Reserve

Chapter Twenty

Baroness Young complimented everyone on the enhancement of this valuable natural resource and said, *"I know you get a lot of human visitors and the wildlife has obviously voted with its feet by being present."*

She went on to say *"Two weeks ago DEFRA published a survey of the UK's natural ecosystems, looking at the value of inland waterways and green spaces to the economy and the wellbeing of the population. They estimated that having a green view nearby was worth £300 a year to each person, so green spaces are officially good value. With changes in climate it is vital that there is a network of natural sites across the country to ensure that our wildlife continues to flourish. Stotfold Watermill Nature Reserve is right on the cutting edge."*

On Tuesday, 25th October 2011, HRH the Duke of Kent, accompanied by Sir Samuel Whitbread, Lord Lieutenant of Bedfordshire, visited Stotfold Watermill and Nature Reserve and met many of the volunteers working to ensure that the Mill and Nature Reserve are sustainable. During his time in the watermill The Duke was given a guided tour, with each area being explained to him by a volunteer specialist. He said, *"The restored Mill is a wonderful testament to the huge communal effort that has gone into turning a near derelict building into the superb working watermill of today"*. Before leaving, he signed the Visitors' Book and was presented with a painting by

The Duke of Kent being presented with an original Geoff Hoile painting by the artist, with Trust Chairman, John Saunders looking on

local artist Geoff Hoile, showing the old derelict building and the new Mill 'risen from the ashes'.

Having completed his tour of the watermill he then visited the adjoining Nature Reserve to see the work that has been done to transform this once desolate pasture and wetlands into the award-winning Local Nature Reserve it is today. Paul Redwood, Chair of the Nature Reserve Management Group, said *"All the comments made by The Duke were very supportive. He had nothing but praise for what had been achieved and commented that the site was very rugged and not over-managed and looked as it should for the time of year"*. The Mayor of Stotfold, Councillor Brian Collier, stated, *"We are extremely proud that Stotfold Watermill and Nature Reserve are seen as a great asset to the area and are delighted that the Lord Lieutenant chose this as one of the sites for the Duke of Kent to visit while in this part of the country."*

In June 2012, the Nature Reserve gained the prestigious Green Flag Award – the national standard for parks and green spaces in the UK. The scheme is also seen as a way of encouraging others to achieve high environmental standards, setting a benchmark of excellence in recreational green areas. This national award recognised the quality of the work put in to the Nature Reserve by volunteers and the value of the area to local residents.

The hard work and dedication of the large number of Mill and Nature Reserve volunteers will continue to ensure that both the Mill and Nature Reserve remain as excellent examples of painstaking craftsmanship and community involvement.

INDEX

Ackroyd, Saul	96, 138, 146
Anderson, Elizabeth (Liz)	96
Andrews, Cliff	90, 92
Antipater,	7
Archer, Sheila	5, 131, 154-156, 158-161
Archive Team	78, 97, 99, 102, 106, 146
Arlesey Road	16
Arlesey White Bricks	51
Arnold, George	67, 68, 70
Astwick Mill	11
Baker, David	6
Balderstone, Kevin	85, 119-120, 122, 124, 136, 140-141
Balderstone, Valerie	v, 88-89, 91, 96
Barker, Sandra	90
Barrow, Julia	153-154, 157
Barrow, Mick	152
Barrow, Simon	133, 136-137, 140-141
Barry, Sue	158
Beale, Nora	96
Beale, Tania	77, 128
Bean, Jean	118, 158
Bedfordshire Agricultural Society	14
Bedfordshire County Council	6, 27, 51, 80
Bedfordshire Museum Services	110
Bedfordshire Rural Communities Charity (BRCC)	90-92, 95
Bedstone	7, 63, 67, 70, 150
Bennett, William	9
Biggleswade Chronicle	6
Biggleswade	3, 6, 15, 18, 30, 46, 75-76, 103
Bignell, Lyndsey	95
Bin Floor Or Secret Floor	77-78
Birch, Pamela	103
Bird, Martin	96
Blackbourne, Cherry	111
Blair Atholl Estate	47
Bolter	76-78, 148, 150
Bounds, Geoff	96
Bowman's Mill	18
Brain, Terry	103
Bray, Michael	89
Brayes Manor	8
Brazier, Dean	49
British Trust For Conservation Volunteers (BTCV)	86
Brook Street	16
Brooks, Maureen	158
Brown, John	2
Brown, Linda	146
Buchan, Kara	137, 141
Burton, Joy	111
Bygrave, Sarah	15
Bygrave, Sid	36
Bypass Stream	42
Campaign To Protect Rural England (CPRE)	94, 164, 166
Cane, William	11
Carré, Joel	86, 90
Cave, Joan	155, 158
Central Bedfordshire Council (CBC)	88, 95, 121, 164, 167
Chaff Cutter	76
Chalmers, Heather	36, 44, 55, 66, 90, 150
Chalmers, Patrick	23, 41, 44-45, 50, 87, 89, 91, 95-96, 120, 147, 165
Channon, Zoe	96
Chellew, Dave	41
Chellew, Jan	130
Choudhury, Fatima	110
Clarey, Anne	109-110
Clarey, Pat	85, 96, 107-108, 111, 114, 117, 121, 144
Clarke, Lucy	v, 96, 120-121, 124, 146, 158
Clarke, Sue	94
Clifton, Ilona	138
Clifton, Paul	96, 139
Clutten, Ed	114, 124
Cocks, Walter E	17
Coffey, Pat	114
Cole, Joseph	11
Cole, Martin	36, 52
Collier, Brian	79-82, 84, 121, 169
Collier, Isabel	158
Cooper, Elizabeth	15
Cooper, Peter	2
Corton Steel	54, 58
County Wildlife Status (CWS)	95, 167
Craig, Wendy	158
Crane, Nicholas	164
Crown Wheel	53, 74
Daffarn, Penny	96
Davidson, Jonathan	96
Dawson, Geraldine	102
Dawson, Henry	8
Derbyshire Gritstone	70

Index

Diesel Engine	22, 74
Dilley, Mick	90
Dimmock, Catherine	36
Domesday Book	8
Downey, Cara	144, 146
Dressing Floor	49, 53, 65, 74-77, 82, 148, 151
Dunn, John	42, 52, 58, 61-63, 67-70, 72, 74-76, 149-150, 152
EB Bedfordshire	81
Education Programme	83, 107-109, 111, 144
Einon, Sandra	80
Elliott-Turner, Kate	121
Ellis, Jonathan	138, 140-141
English Heritage	26, 32
Featherstone, Ruth	96
File, Daisy	130
Finch, Richard	96
Finch, Roger	96
Finney, Libby	100
Fisher, Andrea	155-156, 158
Fisher, Ian	89-90
Foskett, Chris	85, 120
Foskett, Gill	155-156, 158
French Burr Stones	53, 67, 71-72, 149
Friend, Anne Marie	158
Friends Of The Mill	115-116
Gault Bricks	10
Gayler, Charles	13
Gentle, Jane	15
Gentle, Mary	15
Gilbird, John	8
Goater, Malcolm	161
Grain Hopper	78
Grantscape	82
Great Spur Wheel	31, 33, 43, 52-53, 60-62, 66, 81
Green Apple Civic Pride Awards	162
Green Flag Award	95, 169
Green Mills Group	111
Green, Dave	96
Greenshields, Alan	113-114, 138
Griffiths, Margaret	146
Guides Team	97, 107, 113-114, 124
Guilbert, John	8
Guilbert, William	8
Gurney, John	9
Gurney, Mary	9
Gurney, Thomas	9, 11
Halton, Steve	164, 167
Hammond, Darren	96

Hayes, Lyn	120
Hayes, Steve	121
Heritage Lottery Fund	82
Hertfordshire Archives And Local Studies	9
Hertfordshire Museum Service	111
Hill, Jean	96, 156, 158
Hogg, William	11
Hoile, Eileen	158
Hoile, Geoff	v, 99, 106, 144, 160-161, 168-169
Hollick, Peter	121
Hollingsworth, Peter	116, 118
Hook, Barbara	161
Hopper	72, 76, 78, 148, 150
Horse	72-74, 131, 148-149
How, Patricia	107
Howard, Judith	121
Howlett, Charles	96
HRH The Duke Of Edinburgh	163
HRH The Duke Of Kent	168
Huckle, Frances	34, 38, 40, 55, 79, 89-91, 96, 165
Huckle, Gordon	v, 5, 23, 40-41, 66, 81
Hugh de Beauchamp, Baron Of Bedford	8
Hursting Floor	150
Hursting Frame	16-17, 41
Hyde, Bert	V, 9, 13
Hyde, Frank	5, 19, 24, 32
Hyde, Jane	36, 80, 86
Hyde, John	iv, 39, 42, 44, 46-47, 49-51, 66, 82-85, 90, 115, 120, 123, 125, 130-133, 135-137, 40-141, 147, 152-153
Hyde, Julie	141
Insurance	11, 56, 91, 137
Ivel Drainage Board (IDB)	42-43, 81, 88
Ivel Valley Conservation Volunteers (IVCV)	86, 90-91
James, Nina	36
James, Peter	39, 147
Johnson, Gertrude Myatt	18
Johnstan Copse	90
Juniper, Tony	166
Keeping, Nigel	2
Kersey, Jean	99, 114, 119, 121, 145, 146, 158
Kilby, Clare	155, 156, 157, 158
Kilby, Ray	52-53, 58, 62, 71, 74-75, 85, 95, 102, 104, 108, 120, 128, 141, 147-150, 152
Kingfisher Gift Shop	125, 128

171

Index

Kirk, Jane	158
Knebworth House	47, 125, 133, 143
Lamb, Andrew	36
Lamb, Joan	36
Lampit, John	17, 54
Lancashire Boiler	13
Law, Alice	158
Law, Sarah	155, 158
Law, Simon	118, 147, 152
Lawrence, Emma	36
Lawrence, Richard	95
Lincoln, Michael	161
Lindsay, Dorothy	35, 131
Lindsell, Robert	11
Lockey, Elizabeth	15
Lockey, Hannah	15, 20
Lonsdale School	108-110
Lorymer, Richard	8
Lyon, Mavis	155-156, 158
Lyon, Reg	111, 113-114, 127
Lyons, Lisa	146
Machell, Marlene	111-112, 114
Machell, Tony	113
Mackin, Paul	2, 3
Major Events Team	98, 116, 123, 135-139, 141
Manfield, Pamela (Pam)	v, 45, 93, 95-97, 114, 117, 120-121, 144, 146
Manor Farm	49
Martin, Paul	83, 107, 153, 159
Martin, Sarah	v, 36, 38
Masterton, Geraldine (Gerry)	36-37, 39, 45, 55, 87, 89-90, 96, 165
Masterton, Louden	v, 34-36, 40-41, 55, 80-82, 84-87, 89-91, 96, 114, 120, 164-165
McIver, Dave	123
McIver, Nicky	146
Medcalf, Neil	56-58, 62, 65-66, 74, 150
Meeks, Keven (Sic)	2
Meredith, Colin	2
Mid Beds District Council	32, 80-81
Mill Cottage	2-3, 25
Mill Green	100, 111
Mill House	1-2, 12-13, 16, 18, 21, 25, 44
Mill Lane	3, 5, 18
Mill Meadows	83, 85-87, 89, 94, 164, 166-167
Miller, Betty	154
Millers Wheel	98-99, 115-121, 145
Mills, John	24, 163
Mills, Samuel	10

Millstones	26, 31, 40, 53, 59, 61-63, 66-67, 70-72, 75-76, 108, 144, 147-148, 150
Milly Mouse	111
Monaghan, Carolyn	v, 99, 101, 104, 106, 125, 127-128, 159, 161
Moore, Helen	114
Morrow, Adrian (Adi)	35, 67, 69, 130
Motorola	50
Muggeridge, Helen	138, 156, 158
Munns, Jane	111
Museums Education Forum	110
Musselwhite, Jenny	125-126, 128, 161
Mutton, Madeleine	96
Myhill, Marianne	96, 158
Naisbitt, Tim	137, 139
National Mills Weekend	44, 50, 130-131
Newham, Gerry	96
Noble, Dalice	62, 81
Noble, Jerry	62
Norman, Gerry	49
Norman, Stuart	42
NTL	41
O'Brien, Matthew	164
Oat Roller	53, 75-76
Ormerod, Anthony	121
Osborn, Geoff	136-139, 141
Osborn, Jan	133, 135, 141
Oxley, Jenny	100
Papertrail	111
Pateman, Mary	115-116, 133, 136-137, 139
Peacock, Pam	138, 141
Pearson, Doug	100, 114, 121, 142
Pelter, Sue	158
Pestell, James	10
Pit Wheel	17, 30-31, 52-53, 57-60, 63
Plaiting Industry	14-15
Plaster Of Paris	67
Prutton, Jean	155-158
Queen Street	14, 16, 21
Queen's Award For Voluntary Service (QAVC)	117, 165
Quint, Reverend Pat	51
Radford, Jackie	35, 55, 120, 165
Radford, Jan	v, 38-40, 85, 114, 120, 131-132, 165
Radford, Phillip (Phil)	35, 36, 39, 50, 52, 54, 56, 58, 67-68, 70, 72-73, 75-78, 81, 82, 85, 108-109, 120, 147, 150, 152, 165

Index

Radford, Trevor (Trev) V, 34, 38-39, 42, 45, 56, 58, 61, 67-70, 72, 76-77, 81, 82, 90, 120, 129-132, 144, 152, 165
Radwell Grange 16
Radwell Mill 10, 17, 61
Radwell 10, 16-17, 20, 23, 61, 148
Randall, Charles 19
Randall, Ebenezer 17
Randall, Frederick George (George) 23, 50, 71, 80
Randall, John 13-15, 18, 152
Randall, Malvene 82
Randall, Mary 14
Randall, Maud Lilla 19
Randall, Ruth Hilda (Ruth) 46
Randall, Samuel Leslie (Sam) 5, 23-25, 36, 38, 49-50, 54, 67, 70-71, 74, 81, 163
Randall, William 19
Randall's Mill 8, 19, 20, 21
Randalls Tea Room 13, 44, 48, 71, 78-79, 83, 98, 106-107, 109-110, 112, 125, 127, 130, 142-143, 152-161
Ravenall, Olivia 158
Ray, Jan 111
Ray, Lindsay 146
Ray, Tom 85
Redwood, Joyce 119, 158
Redwood, Paul 83-84, 88, 91, 94-96, 103, 107, 117-118, 120, 125, 142, 155, 164, 166, 169
Rennie, John 161
Reynolds, Keith v, 90, 96, 99-101, 106
Reynolds, Lindsay 96, 158
Richardson, June 158
Rickson, Jane 164, 167
Riley, Jenny 161
River Ivel vii, 6, 8, 12-13, 43, 55, 81, 91-92, 153
River Rhee 13
Rodford, Glenn 147, 151-152
Roecroft Academy 108
Roller Mill 18, 23, 25, 31, 34, 39, 44, 46, 74, 79
Rook Tree Lane 19, 29, 41
Roper, Kevin 36
Roper, Lynn v, 34-35, 38, 118, 165
Roper, Ron V, 24-25, 27-28, 31-32, 34, 36, 52, 54, 56-58, 60, 62, 66-67, 70-73, 80-82, 84, 120-121, 147, 151-152, 165-166
Roper, Simon 36
Roper, Tracy 36
Runner Stone 67, 71, 148, 151
Rutherford, Ian 139

Rutherford, Keryle 139, 158
Sack Hoist 4, 26, 31, 53, 74-75, 78, 106, 148, 150
Sarl, William 13, 152
Saunders, Brenda 155, 156, 158
Saunders, Brian 114
Saunders, John 29-30, 32, 42, 51, 74, 80-82, 85, 101, 120, 133, 154, 168
Shepherd, Debbie 138, 141
Shepherd, George 20
Shoe 73, 148
Sluice 42-43, 56, 72, 149
Small Events Team 98, 116, 145-146
Smith, Christine 82, 84-85, 115, 120-121, 125, 127, 130, 132, 135, 137, 141, 143-144, 146, 166
Smith, Francis 8
Smith, Robert v, 113-114, 136, 139, 141, 144
Society For The Protection Of Ancient Buildings (SPAB), Mills Section 25-27, 29-30, 45, 49, 51, 61, 66, 162
South East Beds Community Forum 81
Speltinckx, Julie 104
St Christopher's 108
St Francis College 107-108, 111
St Thomas More Roman Catholic Primary School (St Thomas More) 107-108
Standring, Damien 2
Stanford Mill 15
Stanistreet, Stan 90
Steam Engine 13, 30-31, 74
Steam Fair And Country Show 97, 116, 123, 129, 133, 136, 138, 144, 153, 157
Steele, Martin 2
Stevenson, Freda 3, 24, 34-35, 81
Stevenson, John 34
Stone Floor 24-25, 61-62, 70, 73-74, 112-113
Stone Furniture 31, 72-73, 149
Stone Jacks 61
Stone Nuts 30, 53, 60-63, 152
Stoter, Larry V, 93, 95
Stotfold Art Group 98, 153, 159
Stotfold Carnival Committee 81
Stotfold Cemetery 19-20
Stotfold Mill Nature Reserve vii, 85-87, 90-98, 108, 111-112, 119, 121, 130, 142-144, 160-162, 167-169

173

Index

Stotfold Mill Preservation Trust 32-33, 79, 86
Stotfold Watermill (Stotfold Mill) vii, 1, 2, 8, 11-13, 16, 18, 22, 25-27, 31-33, 37, 51, 61, 72, 74, 77, 79, 86, 92, 93-94, 104, 111, 124, 127, 141, 147, 151, 162-164, 166-169
Stotfold News 116
Stotfold Reflections 20
Stotfold Riots 14
Stotfold Stocks 10, 49
Stotfold Town Council 16, 32-33, 80-81, 91, 95, 121
Stoyel, Alan 6, 25-26, 30, 45, 51, 162
Street, John 80-82, 85, 88, 163
Support Help And Advice From Renaissance England (SHARE) 8-9, 93, 99-101, 111, 114, 139

Tasker, Julian 1
Tasker, Lorelie 1-2, 5, 28, 33, 44, 67, 80, 82, 87, 125, 130, 165
Tasker, Robin v, 1, 29-30, 32, 39, 46, 80-82, 84, 88, 153, 159
Tasker, Roxane 1, 2
Tasker, Tamlin 36
Taylor, John 11, 13
Teasel 32, 85-86, 88-91, 95-96, 98, 107, 119-120, 164
Teer, Nick 2
Templeman, Isabella 8
Tempsford Mill 12
Tentering Gear 59, 61, 70
Thiele, Claudia 108
Thomas, Mike v, 86, 89-90, 95
Thorp, Peter 8
Three Counties Asylum 19
Topping Out Ceremony 50
Towler, Andrew 116
Towler, Jo 117
Trulock, Joan 158
Tun 53, 72-73, 148, 150
Turner, Christina 121
Turner, Tricia 121
Tye, Nicholas 167

Varty And Company 13
Vass, Roger 36
Vaughan, John James 13
Vaughan, William 13, 16
Vaughan, William Thomas 13
Vauxhall Griffin Award 81
Vernon, Joan 158
Vitruvius 7
Vooght-Rogers, Helen 96

Waghorn, Gemma 93
Waldock, David 13
Waldock, George 11-12
Waldock, Henry 12
Wallower 53, 57, 59-63, 152
Waterwheel 7, 11, 16-17, 26, 28, 30-31, 33, 36, 38, 42-44, 53-54, 56-60, 63, 66, 82, 109, 130, 149
Watson, Roger v, 96, 99-102, 106, 117-118, 121
Weathervane 50
Webster, Chris 22, 121, 130-131, 155, 158
Wedewessen, Alice 8
Wedewesssen, John 8
Welwyn Thalians 130
Werrett, Bob 104
Werrett, Carol 103
Weston, Peter 46-47
Wheatcroft, Dave 36
Wheatcroft, Wendy 36
Whitbread KCVO, Sir Samuel 121, 165
Whitelock, Richard v, 99, 106, 136, 139, 152, 161
Whiteway, Emma 144, 146
Whitmore and Binyon 17, 26, 31, 59, 61
Whitty, Clare 89, 96, 107, 109, 111, 114
Wilding, Linda 158
Wildlife Watch Group (Watch Group) 93
Winnower 53, 148
Woodrow, Brian 121
Woods, Hilary 114, 146
Woodward, James 8
Working Steam Weekend 97-98, 103, 116, 131, 138, 140
Wrayfields 10, 23, 36, 49
Wren 82

Young of Old Scone, Baroness 94, 167